Key Terms in Philosophy of Mind

Continuum *Key Terms in Philosophy*

The *Key Terms* series offers undergraduate students clear, concise, and accessible introductions to core topics. Each book includes a comprehensive overview of the key terms, concepts, thinkers, and texts in the area covered and ends with a guide to further resources.

Key Terms in Philosophy forthcoming from Continuum:

Aesthetics, Brent Kalar
Ethics, Oskari Kuusela
Logic, edited by Jon Williamson and Federica Russo
Philosophy of Religion, Raymond J. VanArragon
Political Philosophy, Jethro Butler

Key Terms in Philosophy of Mind

Pete Mandik

continuum

Continuum International Publishing Group

The Tower Building
11 York Road
London SE1 7NX

80 Maiden Lane
Suite 704
New York, NY 10038

www.continuumbooks.com

British Library Cataloguing-in-Publication Data
A catalogue record for this book is available from the British Library.

ISBN: HB: 978-1-8470-6348-9
      PB: 978-1-8470-6349-6

Library of Congress Cataloging-in-Publication Data
A catalog record for this book is available from the Library of Congress.

Typeset by Newgen Imaging Systems Pvt Ltd, Chennai, India
Printed and bound in Great Britain by the MPG Books Group

Contents

Acknowledgments

For valuable comments on early draft versions of several of the entries, I am grateful to the following individuals: Ken Aizawa, Anibal Astobiza, James Dow, Tanasije Gjorgoski, Peter Hankins, Bryce Huebner, Corey Maley, Marcin Milkowski, Liz Schier, Eric Schwitzgebel, Eric Steinhart, Eric Thomson, Gary Williams, and Chase Wrenn.

For love, support, and very serious and thorough assistance with the text based on a mastery of the English language that is far superior to my own, I thank my wife, Rachelle Mandik.

Introduction: What Is Philosophy of Mind?

The topics definitive of the philosophy of mind, such as the MIND/BODY PROBLEM, INTENTIONALITY, CONSCIOUSNESS, and THE PROBLEM OF OTHER MINDS, are problems of enormous importance to broader philosophical concerns in the main branches of philosophy: metaphysics, ethics, and EPISTEMOLOGY. Here are some brief descriptions of intersections of central concern between philosophy of mind and, respectively, metaphysics, ethics, and epistemology. (Note that small capital letters are used throughout this book for cross-referencing between the many entries.)

Metaphysics: Core questions of existence concern the nature and extent of both mind-dependent and mind-independent existence.

Ethics: Beings who have moral standing and to whom ethical obligations are directed are beings with minds, as are the beings with the obligations.

Epistemology: Various key means by which knowledge is gained, such as PERCEPTION, INTROSPECTION, and INFERENCE, are mental faculties. Further, special problems arise concerning minds as objects of knowledge: how, for example, can it be known whether there are minds other than my own?

Philosophy of mind thus plays a central role in the broad philosophical project of understanding reality, our place and (moral) status within it, and the means by which such understanding is achieved.

In addition to intersections with other key areas of philosophy, philosophy of mind has also enjoyed prominent interactions with various empirical sciences in recent decades, especially through interdisciplinary interactions with the cognitive sciences (*see* COGNITIVE SCIENCE). Thus, much recent work in philosophy of mind has been informed by (and to some extent, has informed) advances in psychology, linguistics, ARTIFICIAL INTELLIGENCE, neuroscience, and anthropology.

Because of the various interactions philosophy of mind has enjoyed, both inside the broader discipline of philosophy and outside of it, contemporary philosophers of mind employ a rich vocabulary of technical terms often borrowed and adapted from other fields. Such terminological richness can be more a burden than a boon to the novice. And even readers beyond the novice level may welcome guidance through the thicket of terms and ideas that make up the philosophy of mind. The remainder of this introductory essay lays out foundational problems that define the contemporary philosophy of mind.

The mind/body problem

Since so many of the historical and contemporary discussions in the philosophy of mind concern what has come to be known as "the mind/body problem," we do well to start here with our introduction to the philosophy of mind.

An inventory of our world would likely mention the many physical bodies that apparently populate it. Such bodies include more than just the bodies of people and nonhuman animals, but stones, coffee cups, and crumpled pieces of paper count among the physical bodies as well. Physical bodies exemplify characteristically physical properties, properties such as their shape, mass, and electrical charge (*see* PROPERTY).

Arguably, physical bodies and their physical properties aren't the only entities or phenomena that we encounter in attempting the world's inventory. We are aware of much else besides, in particular, our AWARENESS itself may count among the existing things, and the properties of our own awareness may count among the properties instantitated (*see* INSTANTIATION). Perhaps each of us is identical to or at least in possession of a special nonphysical entity in virtue of which we are aware. Call this alleged entity a "mind." As a first stab at characterizing the mind/body problem, it is the problem of specifying whether there are such things as minds, such properties as mental properties, and, if so, specifying the nature of any relations that mental things and properties bear to physical bodies and physical properties.

Some philosophers argue that minds and/or mental properties are radically distinct from physical bodies and their properties. Such positions comprise the various kinds of DUALISM. One kind of dualism, substance dualism (*see* DUALISM, SUBSTANCE), involves viewing the world as populated by two radically distinct kinds of particulars. According to the substance dualism promoted by René DESCARTES, physical particulars are things that essentially have EXTENSION (the capacity to occupy space) and essentially lack the capacity for thinking, whereas mental particulars are things that are essentially thinking and unextended.

A little later, we'll examine two special aspects of mentality, intentionality, and consciousness, each of which results in distinctive sets of considerations regarding the mind/body problem. But for now, we can continue our focus on Descartes's approach to the mind/body problem. For Descartes, one of the ideas that helped prove the distinctness of his mind and his body was the idea that his own mind was known by him for certain to exist (since not even a powerful demon could deceive him about the truth of propositions like "I think," "I exist," and "I am a thinking thing"), while no such certainty, however, attached to propositions concerning the existence of *any* physical body (since, for all Descartes knows, a powerful demon may very well be fooling him about those propositions).

Problems raised for Cartesian substance dualism include the problem of whether there's any good argument for it and whether it is compatible with the commonsense view that there are causal interactions between the mental and the physical. Such commonsense causal interactions include when a physical event (such as an explosion) causes the (mental) perception of it or when a (mental) volitional or intentional state results in a physical event (such as a ball being kicked). This latter problem that arises for Cartesian dualism—the *problem of interaction*—is the problem of explaining how entities as allegedly diverse as differing in whether they even have spatial extent can nonetheless enter into causal relationships (*see* MENTAL CAUSATION).

Slightly different dualisms posit that instead of a mental/physical divide between kinds of particulars, a mental/physical divide between kinds of properties that may be had by a single particular. This latter variety of dualism—property dualism (*see* DUALISM, PROPERTY)—may nonetheless be prone to its own version of the problem of interaction, since questions may be raised in terms of the causal efficacy of properties, and thus, for example, the question arises of whether a particular's nonphysical mental properties can be causally efficacious with respect to the distribution of nonmental physical properties in the world.

While some philosophers attempt to either fix or live with the problems of dualism, others reject dualism, embracing instead one of the various forms of monism. One general form of monism—MATERIALISM or PHYSICALISM—embraces the view that everything is ultimately physical. Two kinds of physicalists are reductive physicalists (*see* PHYSICALISM, REDUCTIVE) who affirm the identification of mental phenomena with certain kinds of physical phenomena and eliminative materialists (*see* ELIMINATIVE MATERIALISM) who deny the existence of anything mental. Another kind of monism—IDEALISM—embraces the view that everything is ultimately mental and so-called physical bodies such as rocks, coffee cups, and crumpled pieces of paper have no existence independent of our perceptions or ideas of them. Noneliminativist physicalist monism is the most popular alternative to dualism embraced by contemporary philosophers of mind, though these physicalists are divided among themselves over how best to conceive mental/physical relations. One position in this area—FUNCTIONALISM—holds that mental states are multiply realizable in such diverse systems as biological nervous systems and appropriately programmed electronic computers (*see* MULTIPLE REALIZABILITY). In contrast, many *identity theorists* (*see* TYPE-IDENTITY THESIS) affirm that mental states are identical to brain states and thus nothing lacking a biological brain could instantiate the mental states instantiated by humans.

The discussion so far has made little mention of the properties alleged by some philosophers to be special properties of mental states, properties such as intentionality and consciousness. It is to such properties and their relevance to the mind/body problem that we now turn.

Intentionality

Intentionality may be characterized as the directedness of the mind upon its objects, but intentionality is too puzzling and this characterization too brief for justice to thereby be done. Many philosophers would offer as core examples of mental states with intentionality the various mental states that can be described as being *about* something. Thus would a THOUGHT about a vacation in Paris or a BELIEF about the average temperature on the surface of Mars exhibit intentionality or "aboutness." The puzzling nature of intentionality may be highlighted by focusing on mental states that are about things or states of affairs that are so remote from us in space and/or time that we are unable to have had any causal interaction with them. How is it possible for us to think about, for example, things in regions of space so far away that, given the limit of the speed of light, there is no sort of physical-causal relation that we can bear to things in those distant regions? The puzzling nature of intentionality may be even more acutely felt upon contemplation of thoughts about things and states of affairs (*see* STATE OF AFFAIRS) that don't even exist. On the face of it, it seems that people are quite capable of thinking of nonexistent things like the fountain of youth and unicorns and nonobtaining states of affairs like Luke Skywalker's destruction of the Death Star or that one time when Barack Obama flew to the moon by flapping his arms.

One way to put a point on what's puzzling about intentionality is to regard the problem of intentionality as an inconsistent triad of propositions, each of which is compelling, at least when considered in isolation.

1. We can think about things that do not exist.
2. Intentionality is a relation between a thinker and a thing thought about.
3. We can bear relations only to things that exist.

It should be apparent that if (1) and (2) are true, then (3) must be false; if (1) and (3) are true, then (2) must be false; and if (2) and (3) are true, then (1) must be false.

If one is to eliminate contradictory beliefs, then one must deny the truth of at least one of these three propositions. However, it is difficult to see which is the most eliminable, since each is independently plausible. It's hard to see, for instance, how (1) can be coherently denied, since understanding the denial arguably involves thinking that *there exist no thoughts of things that don't exist*, which in turn involves thinking of things alleged not to exist—namely, a certain kind of thought.

The attractiveness of proposition (2) may be highlighted by focusing on thoughts of things that *do* exist. I take it as relatively uncontroversial that this book exists. At least on the face of it, it seems plausible that as I think thoughts like the thought that *this is a book written by me*, I am entering into a relation with this book. It is plausible to suppose that what makes it the case that I'm thinking about this book right now and not some other entity is that there is some special *relation* that I bear to this book and to no other entity. If proposition (2) is denied, then it is hard to see what sense can be made of claims like "this is the book I am thinking about."

Regarding proposition (3), it seems compelling especially when we focus on relations between physical objects. My coffee cup bears a relation of containment to the coffee inside of it and bears a relation to my desk of being on top of it. My coffee cup, however, cannot contain nonexistent beverages (it would instead be empty and contain nothing) and cannot be set on nonexistent surfaces (it would instead be unsupported and fall to the floor).

The problem of intentionality has inspired some philosophers to embrace a kind of dualism whereby intentionality involves a special nonphysical relation that thinkers bear to a special nonphysical realm of entities that, despite not existing, have a different mode of being that we might call "SUBSISTENCE" or "INEXISTENCE." Other philosophers have struggled to construct theories whereby intentionality is fully consistent with a physicalist worldview (see CONTENT, THEORIES OF).

Consciousness

Intentionality is not the only aspect of the mind that makes the mind/body problem especially problematic. We turn now to consider problems concerning consciousness. Many philosophers see consciousness as raising problems distinct from the problems of intentionality, and we can begin to appreciate this distinctness with the following remarks: You have likely believed for quite a long time, probably many years, that the English alphabet has twenty-six letters in it. This belief is a mental STATE with intentionality, since it is a mental state that is *about* something. It is about the number of letters in the English alphabet. While you were in possession of this intentional state for many years, it is highly unlikely that it was a *conscious* mental state for that entire duration. It is highly unlikely that you've been *consciously* entertaining the proposition that the alphabet has twenty-six letters during the whole time that you've believed this proposition.

For the above reasons, beliefs, which are prototypical instances of states that exhibit intentionality, are *not* prototypical instances of states that exhibit consciousness. According to some, prototypical instances of conscious states would include sensory experiences (see EXPERIENCE), such as feeling an intense pain, tasting a zesty lemon, or seeing a bright red light. Such states exhibit what philosophers call QUALIA, or phenomenal qualities. These philosophers characterize qualia as the properties of experiences in virtue of which there is *something it's like* to have experiences (see WHAT IT IS LIKE).

Phrases such as "knowing what it's like" and "there is something that it's like" play a large role in philosophical discussions of consciousness. To get a feel for this role, contemplate the questions of whether (1) you know what it's like to jump out of an airplane, (2) a person blind from birth can know what it's like to see red, and (3) tasting a lemon is more like tasting a lime than it is like tasting chocolate. Thinking about the questions raised here involves understanding the "what it's like" phrase in ways pertinent to discussions of consciousness and the qualities of experience.

The notion of what it's like has been marshaled in various lines of thought against physicalism. One line of thought is that knowing the physical properties of a conscious being can never suffice, no matter how many physical facts are known, for knowledge of what it's like to be a bat or what it's like to see red. If, for example, all physical facts can be known by a color-blind person who doesn't know what it's like to see red, then, arguably, facts about what it's like to see red can't be physical facts (see KNOWLEDGE ARGUMENT).

Another line of thought against physicalism based on *what it's like* involves thought experiments (see THOUGHT EXPERIMENT) concerning beings *physically* similar to each other but nonetheless dissimilar with respect to what it's like to be them. In the INVERTED SPECTRUM thought experiment, one is to imagine a being *physically* similar to oneself even though what it's like for the being when he or she visually experiences *red* objects is like what it's like for *you* to experience *green* objects and vice versa. In the ZOMBIE thought experiment, one is to imagine a being physically similar to oneself but for whom there is nothing it's like to be. That is, zombies are phenomenally vacant and there is no more anything it is like to be a zombie than there is anything it is like to be a rock.

Arguably, if inverted spectra or zombies are imaginable, then they are possible and if they are possible, then properties concerning what it's like must be distinct from physical properties. (See IMAGINATION; CONCEIVABILITY; POSSIBILITY.) Thus have zombies and inverted spectra figured in arguments against physicalism.

Considerable controversy surrounds the question of whether there are sound arguments against physicalism and contemporary physicalists have expended considerable effort in attempting to show how consciousness is consistent with a physicalist worldview after all. (See MODAL ARGUMENT; EXPLANATORY GAP.)

Other problems

While the mind/body problem looms large in the philosophy of mind, it is not the only problem. In the remainder of this introductory essay, we will review problems concerning (1) perception, (2) other minds, (3) the relation of language to thought, (4) mental imagery, and (5) free will.

The problem of perception concerns questions such as "*What* do we perceive?" and "*How* do we perceive it?" The position of DIRECT REALISM is that *what* we perceive are physical objects such as coffee cups and crumpled pieces of paper and *how* we perceive them is via a *direct* relation between the perceiver and the perceived. Understanding this claim of directness is perhaps best done by appreciating the opposing view of INDIRECT REALISM aka REPRESENTATIONAL REALISM. According to this view, we perceive physical objects only indirectly via our direct perception of our *ideas* or mental representations (*see* MENTAL REPRESENTATION) of physical objects. According to one version of indirect realism, I directly perceive my *idea* of a coffee cup—an entity (the idea) internal to my mind—and then draw an inference that my current idea of a coffee cup is caused by a real coffee cup external to my mind. Such a view, however, leads to skeptical worries of whether we can ever *know* that there are physical objects (*see* SKEPTICISM).

No matter how the knowledge of physical objects is accounted for, it seems to be a separate problem altogether about how we know of the existence of other minds. One way of raising the problem of other minds is by starting with the presupposition that I know my own mind by direct awareness via introspection and when I turn my attention to the world outside of my mind, I seem restricted to perceiving various physical bodies; I don't introspect or perceive any other mind. A serious question thus arises of whether any of those bodies, even the bodies of living humans, have minds. How do I know that they aren't instead total zombies devoid of qualia and intentionality? According to the *argument by analogy*, I reason that since certain of *my* mental states, such as joy, are associated with certain of *my* bodily behaviors, such as smiling, it follows by analogy that when the bodies of *other* humans *act* joyous it is because they *really are* joyous (*see* ACTION). I reason, by analogy, that the other person, like me, has a mind. A big problem with the argument by analogy, however, is that it constitutes the hastiest of generalizations: It involves making a generalization about *all* humans based on an observation of only a single case, namely, my own case.

Some philosophers have sought to resolve the problem of other minds and avoid the pitfalls of the argument by analogy by questioning the premise that there is a disanalogy between our knowledge of our own minds and the minds of others. In particular, they question whether our minds are constituted by private phenomena to which each of us has sole and direct access to. More broadly, some philosophers question whether we have FIRST-PERSON AUTHORITY regarding our own mental states. The philosopher Ludwig WITTGENSTEIN pressed such a line of questioning by developing what has come to be known as the PRIVATE LANGUAGE ARGUMENT. While controversy surrounds the question of exactly what Wittgenstein's argument is, we may sketch it as follows.

If my mental events are private events of which I am uniquely aware, it ought to be possible for there to be a private language with which I refer to such events. However, the very idea of a language with which one can refer presupposes the idea of publicly evaluable norms of application (*see* NORMATIVE). In other words, it has to make sense to say whether I've correctly or incorrectly applied a term to something, and this can only make sense in a community wherein norms are devised and enforced. However, an allegedly private language is one for which it wouldn't even make sense for me, let alone anyone else, to raise the question of whether I've used it correctly on any particular occasion.

Whatever the merits of the proposal that there can be a *private* language, there are further questions concerning the relations between language and thought that have intrigued philosophers of mind. One interesting proposal is that thought itself is a kind of language. Part of what is involved in postulating a LANGUAGE OF THOUGHT is the claim that thoughts have their intentionality in a way that is distinctive of languages as opposed to, for instance, the intentionality that might be exhibited by pictures. Plausibly, pictures function by resembling what they are pictures of. However, items in a language, such as descriptions, do not need to resemble the things they describe in anything like the way that pictures resemble what they depict.

Relevant to the evaluation of such issues is the question of what the nature of so-called mental images is (*see* IMAGERY). Imagining an apple may be more similar to seeing an apple than saying "apple," but it nonetheless may be questioned whether the mental state is more like a picture (a thing that represents an apple in virtue of sharing certain properties with an apple) or a set of one or more words.

Another aspect of mentality that has been of special interest to philosophers concerns VOLITION and the will (*see* WILL, THE). Some of the things going on in the world are more than mere happenings. They are actions of AGENTS. Mindless entities may move and be moved, but, some philosophers claim, only entities with minds do what they *will*. A central issue that arises here is whether there is such a thing as FREE WILL. Are we the authors of our actions? Are our actions caused and thus predetermined? If so, is determinism compatible with our actions being willed freely? The problem of free will intersects at various points with the mind-body problem. If physicalism is true and all physical events have only physical causes, what room is there in such a system for freedom and responsibility?

This introductory essay has barely scratched the surface of all that comprises the field of philosophy of mind. But in showing the key features of some of the field's main concerns, I hope to have provided some useful orientation for further explorations conducted by both students and experts.

The Key Terms

action, a kind of EVENT, distinctive for the essential role played by an AGENT—namely, that the event is something done or performed *by* the agent and *not*, for instance, something that merely happens *to* the agent. To illustrate: if I step out into the cold without a jacket and subsequently begin shivering, my stepping out into the cold without a jacket is an *action* I perform, whereas my shivering is something that merely *happens* to me. It is one of the central concerns of the area of philosophy known as ACTION THEORY to supply an account of what distinguishes actions from mere happenings. Part of what makes it difficult to supply a general account of action is the heterogeneity of what counts as an action: in addition to actions concerning bodily motions (climbing a ladder, arching one's eyebrow) there are also exclusively mental actions (calculating a sum "in one's head") as well as negative actions (refraining from doing something rude). Restricting attention to actions involving bodily motions, one way that has appealed to some philosophers of accounting for the distinction between actions involving bodily motions (deliberately kicking a ball) and bodily motions that are mere happenings (involuntarily sneezing upon inadvertently inhaling some dust) is that only actions are (directly) caused by mental states. For example, what makes the kicking of the ball an action is its having as a cause the pairing of a DESIRE to score a goal in a soccer game and a BELIEF that such a maneuver would help score a goal. However, such a causal analysis of action is not entirely uncontroversial. One sort of problem that such an analysis encounters concerns *deviant causal chains*: bodily motions that are the causal consequences of mental states yet do not thereby count as actions. In one such example, a mountain climber who is planning to kill his partner during an expedition gets sweaty hands as a result of contemplating committing the murder and accidentally loses grip of a rope, thereby sending the partner to his death. While there's a sense in which the death was a causal consequence of the would-be murderer's INTENTION to kill, the incident of the intervening sweaty hands seems to prevent the caused death from counting as an intentional killing. *See also* INTENTIONAL ACTION; WEAKNESS OF WILL; WILL, THE.

action theory, an area of philosophy dedicated to the investigation of topics related to ACTION, such as being an AGENT; INTENTIONAL ACTION; WEAKNESS OF WILL; WILL, THE.

adverbialism, a theory of PERCEPTION consistent with DIRECT REALISM that attempts to avoid committing to perceptual intermediaries such as SENSE-DATA by giving adverbial paraphrases such as (1) "John sensed red-ly" in place of both (2) "John sensed a red datum" and (3) "John sensed a red thing." On the face of it, (2) and (3) each commits the speaker to the existence of two entities: John and the red thing he senses. But this is highly problematic, especially since (2) and (3) can arguably be true even though John is undergoing a hallucination of a red thing (*see* ARGUMENT FROM ILLUSION). One of the problems raised against adverbialism is the difficulty presented in accounting for statements such as (4) "John saw a red square and a blue circle." The problem here raised is that the most straightforward adverbial paraphrase is (5) "John saw red-ly, bluely, squarely, and circle-ly," which seems inadequate to capture (4), since it may just as well be the adverbial paraphrase for the following statement logically distinct from (4), (6) "John saw a blue square and a red circle." *See also* SENSE-DATUM THEORY; REPRESENTATIVE REALISM.

agent, a being possessing the capacity for ACTION.

akrasia, Greek term roughly translatable as WEAKNESS OF WILL. Akrasia was one of the main topics discussed by ARISTOTLE in his *Nicomachean Ethics*.

anomalous monism, a variety of MONISM, specifically a kind of MATERIALISM or PHYSICALISM, due to Donald DAVIDSON wherein it is affirmed that each TOKEN mental EVENT is identical to a token physical event, but that while there are *physical* laws and nomic (i.e., lawful) relations that events enter into, there are no *psychological* laws or nomic relations that they enter into. *See also* PHYSICALISM, NONREDUCTIVE; TOKEN-IDENTITY THESIS; SUPERVENIENCE.

appearance, a way in which something *seems*, as distinct from the way it really *is*.

Issues surrounding the distinction between appearance and REALITY have been crucial in many areas of philosophy, but of special interest to philosophers of mind are issues surrounding sensory or sensible appearances: the ways in which things appear to sensory PERCEPTION. The ways things appear to vision, hearing, touch, olfaction, and taste are, respectively, the way things look, sound, feel, smell, and taste. Philosophers of mind have been curious about whether sensory appearances should be regarded as a special and irreducible feature of reality. See, in connection with such a line of thought, the entry on QUALIA.

One kind of claim that some philosophers have made about sensory appearances is that they are distinct from most, if not all, other things for not themselves admitting of a distinction between appearance and reality. In other words, the reality of a sensory appearance is exhausted by the way it appears. Such a philosopher might claim that whereas it makes sense to distinguish between the way a rock seems and the way a rock really is, there is no analogous distinction between the way the rock seems and the way the rock seems to seem. KRIPKE and others have made a similar sort of remark about pain: there is nothing more to a mental state's *being* a pain (its reality) than its *seeming* painful (its appearance) (*see* MODAL ARGUMENT).

Another kind of claim that some philosophers have made about sensory appearances is that they are to be distinguished from a kind of appearance that has less to do with sensory perception and more to do with cognition or the intellect. For so-called *epistemic appearances*, the way a thing appears to the mind is reducible (*see* REDUCTION) to a BELIEF one has about the thing. Epistemically, there's nothing more to a rock's appearing igneous to me than my believing it to be igneous. Some philosophers of mind hold that there are two distinct kinds of appearance—phenomenal appearances and epistemic appearances—such that phenomenal appearances are irreducibly sensory and cannot be regarded as reducible to a kind of epistemic appearance.

argument from illusion, a line of reasoning advanced in favor of theories of PERCEPTION such as REPRESENTATIVE REALISM and the SENSE-DATUM THEORY that has as its key premises statements concerning what may broadly be called "illusory" experiences and include, in addition to perceptual illusions, dreams and hallucinations. The following sketch of the argument from illusion will focus on dreams.

It sometimes occurs that one has a dream that is so realistic that, while dreaming, one cannot distinguish the dream experience from an accurate perceptual experience of a real object. Suppose, for example, you are dreaming that you are swimming with a mermaid and you see, in the dream, her long green, scaled tail. In reality, you are at home, safe and dry in bed. There is no mermaid with whom you are in any causal contact. There may not even be anything long and green present in your bedroom. Nonetheless, and here is an important premise of the argument, the dreamer is aware of *something*. Since that something couldn't be a real mermaid's tail, or even a real elongated green object, that something must be some mental item, a SENSE-DATUM or some other form of MENTAL REPRESENTATION. It is this mental item of which the dreamer is directly aware. And since an accurate perception of an actual elongated green object is subjectively indistinguishable from a certain kind of realistic dream, even in the case of an accurate perception of an object in reality, one is aware of that object only indirectly via the mediation of the direct awareness of the inner mental item.

artificial intelligence, the possession by an artifact of the capacity for THOUGHT and REASONING. The phrase "artificial intelligence" may also be used to denote a set of research programs concerned with the creation of such artifacts. The phrases "strong artificial intelligence" and "weak artificial intelligence" have been used by some authors as labels for the respective opposing positions that artificial systems may exhibit *genuine* INTELLIGENCE and that artificial systems may only exhibit the mere *appearance* of intelligence (*see* APPEARANCE).

The central philosophical question raised by the prospect of artificial intelligence is "Can a machine think?" Due to the presumption that machines are *physical*, discussion of this central question has been closely tied to discussions of PHYSICALISM. Due to the presumption that machines are made of *different physical stuff* than people are, discussion of the central question has been closely tied to discussions of MULTIPLE REALIZABILITY and FUNCTIONALISM.

A famous philosophical argument against the possibility of strong artificial intelligence is John Searle's CHINESE ROOM argument. See also Ned Block's related CHINESE NATION argument.

The flexibility of programmable computers has made them a natural choice for a set of technologies to press into the service of artificial intelligence. And though a wide availability of computing technology is a relatively recent phenomenon, the suggestion that thought is a kind of COMPUTATION is several hundreds of years old.

There are two predominant schools of thought concerning the best way to achieve artificial intelligent systems comparable to human minds. The first is SYMBOLICISM, which roughly models cognition as the rule-governed manipulation of language-like symbols (*see* LANGUAGE OF THOUGHT). The second is *parallel distributed processing* or CONNECTIONISM, which roughly models cognition as the activity of multiple connected units or "artificial neurons." *See also* GOFAI; TURING TEST.

associationism, the theory that the primary mechanism in learning is one whereby the triggering of one THOUGHT (or idea or behavior) comes to be able to trigger another. One proposed mechanism of association concerns pleasure: if the co-occurrence of two distinct thoughts is accompanied by a feeling of pleasure, then the likelihood is raised that the occurrence of one of the thoughts will suffice for the triggering of the other. Associationist theories of learning were traditionally attractive to empiricists and more recently to behaviorists and connectionists. *See also* EMPIRICISM; BEHAVIORISM; CONNECTIONISM.

atomism, the thesis, contrasted with HOLISM, that mental states have their CONTENT due to factors *other than* whatever relations they may bear to other mental states. Atomism is thus compatible with some theories of content (*see* CONTENT, THEORIES OF) such as versions of the INFORMATIONAL THEORY OF CONTENT and incompatible with other theories of content such as CONCEPTUAL-ROLE SEMANTICS. For a sketch of considerations on either side of the atomism/holism debate, see the entry on HOLISM.

awareness, see CONSCIOUSNESS.

behaviorism, in philosophy, is a position sometimes called "philosophical behaviorism," "logical behaviorism," or "analytical behaviorism" to distinguish it from a view in psychology sometimes called "methodological behaviorism," "psychological behaviorism," or "empirical behaviorism." Empirical behaviorism arose in the early twentieth century in rebellion against an earlier school of thought, *introspectionism*, which viewed CONSCIOUSNESS as the proper object of psychological study and INTROSPECTION as the main means for accessing facts about consciousness. While *empirical* behaviorism is a view about the *methodology* most suited to the scientific study of the mind—namely that it is best done by conducting experiments concerning observable behaviors— *philosophical* behaviorism, which also arose in the early twentieth century, is a view about the *meaning* of commonsense psychological concepts—namely that they can be analyzed in terms of observable behaviors and/or dispositions toward observable behaviors. Alternately, philosophical behaviorism may be formulated as a metaphysical thesis about the nature of mental states—namely that they are identical to certain patterns of observable behaviors and/or dispositions toward observable behaviors.

Early proponents of philosophical behaviorism were logical positivists (*see* LOGICAL POSITIVISM) who adhered to VERIFICATIONISM. If the meaning of a term is constituted by its conditions of verification, and the only way one could verify mental-state ascriptions is via observable behaviors, it would follow that the meanings of mental terms would be specifiable in terms of observable behaviors.

One particularly influential criticism of this behaviorist position is due to Peter Geach, who emphasized that there is no single behavioral expression of a given BELIEF and that what behavior a given belief results in depends on what additional mental states the believer has, including additional beliefs as well as desires (*see* DESIRE). For example, my belief that there is beer in the refrigerator would not alone suffice for my opening the refrigerator. If I additionally lack a desire for beer or additionally have a belief that there is a bomb in the refrigerator with a trigger attached to the door, my belief in a refrigerator full of beer bottles may very well not lead to my opening the fridge. Geach's criticism shows that behavioristically specified verification conditions for the ascription of a single belief would have to be intractably complex.

Other philosophers to develop behaviorist positions included RYLE, WITTGENSTEIN, and QUINE. However, it should be noted that controversy surrounds the question of just *how* behaviorist each philosopher's view really is.

Philosophical and empirical behaviorists share a reluctance to place much emphasis on characterizing mental states in terms of *inner* processes or states of a creature. This de-emphasis on anything that might intervene between observable stimuli and observable responses is distinctively opposed to the historical successors to behaviorism in the philosophy of mind: IDENTITY THEORY and FUNCTIONALISM.

belief, an assertoric PROPOSITIONAL ATTITUDE. An attitude of taking a PROPOSITION to be true.

Many philosophers hold that there are crucial links between belief and language. One apparent link between belief and language is that what one says or expresses in sincerely uttering a declarative sentence is also one of the beliefs that one holds. For instance, if I sincerely utter the English declarative sentence "Grass is green," I thereby express my belief that grass is green. Further, beliefs and items in language both have semantic properties (*see* SEMANTICS). For example, both my belief that there is beer in my refrigerator and the sentence "There is beer in my refrigerator" can have the semantic property of being *true* (*see* TRUTH). Some philosophers have seen the relation between propositional attitudes such as belief and language to be so tight as to posit that one has a belief by having certain sentences occur in one's own LANGUAGE OF THOUGHT.

Beliefs may also figure in the explanation of ACTION. Beliefs can, in concert with desires (*see* DESIRE) and other mental states, serve as both REASONS for and causes of someone's acting in some particular manner. For example, George's opening the refrigerator may be (rationally and causally) explained, at least partially, by reference to his belief that there is beer in the refrigerator and his desire to get some beer. It is characteristic to hold, in many versions of FUNCTIONALISM, that a belief may be definable in terms of the kinds of causal relations that such a state may bear to other mental states, as well as states of sensory input and states of behavioral output.

While belief is to be distinguished from KNOWLEDGE on some views, since false-hoods may be believed but not known, some philosophers hold that belief is an analytic component of, or necessary condition on, knowledge, meaning that *P* can be known only if *P* is believed. *See also* FOLK PSYCHOLOGY; INTENTIONAL STANCE; INTENTIONALITY; REASONS.

black box, an item hypothesized for the explanation of some behavior or function that is characterized in terms of the role that the item plays but, crucially, is *not* characterized in terms of any structures or mechanisms internal to the item that would explain how the item itself works. The imagery of the item being a "black box" suggests that one cannot see into the item to discern how it is that it plays the role it has been hypothesized to play (in contrast, perhaps, to a "glass box"). One way of characterizing FUNCTIONALISM is as decomposing the mind into a collection of interacting black boxes. One way of characterizing BEHAVIORISM is as treating the entire mind as a single black box. One way of characterizing METHODOLOGICAL SOLIPSISM (a characterization attributed to Keith Gunderson) is as a conception of the mind as a glass box in a black world.

blindsight, a neuropsychological condition due to damage to visual areas of the brain, resulting in subjects who report being unable to see things in certain portions of their visual field but nonetheless, under certain tests such as being forced to guess, demonstrate that they do have some ability to process visual INFORMATION from the corresponding regions. In some sense, then, such a subject retains an ability to see what's going on in certain regions of her visual field despite it seeming to her that she is blind to those regions.

Some philosophers of mind have been interested in the implications that blindsight might have for the study of CONSCIOUSNESS. Some have discussed the possibility of a hypothetical condition called "super-blindsight," wherein beings would retain *all* normal functioning with respect to information coming in through their eyes but nonetheless experience no visual consciousness or visual QUALIA. *See also* ZOMBIE.

bottom-up, hypothesized system of processing determining the nature of PERCEPTION wherein what is perceived and the way it is perceived are due largely to INFORMATION coming in through sensory organs. In contrast, perception is hypothesized to be due to *top-down* processing insofar as what is perceived and the way it is perceived are due to so-called higher-level processes such as those underlying MEMORY, CONCEPTS, and THOUGHT. Contrasting against the bottom-up view of perception is the hypothesis of perceptual underdetermination (*see* UNDERDETERMINATION, PERCEPTUAL).

bracketing, a technique in the investigation of PHENOMENOLOGY whereby one suspends judgments about the causes or significance of one's current EXPERIENCE in order to gain KNOWLEDGE concerning the experience itself. Similarly, one might suspend judgments about whatever REALITY lies beyond APPEARANCE in the service of knowledge of appearances themselves.

brain in a vat, a SKEPTICAL HYPOTHESIS wherein one's otherwise normal human brain is disconnected from the rest of the human body and kept alive in a vat of nutrient chemicals and stimulated by electrical connections from a computer that provides a foolproof sensory simulacrum or virtual reality. While epistemologists are interested in what brain-in-a-vat thought experiments (*see* THOUGHT EXPERIMENT) can reveal about our justification for our beliefs in the external world, philosophers of mind are interested in what such thought experiments might reveal about any constitutive relations that mental states may bear to the external world (*see* EXTERNALISM). One sort of position held by some philosophers of mind is that a brain that was always "envatted" would necessarily differ from an embodied brain (*see* EMBODIED COGNITION) with respect to the CONTENT of some of its PROPOSITIONAL ATTITUDES but may nonetheless have all of the same QUALIA associated with its sensory experiences.

The philosopher Hilary PUTNAM developed an argument against the hypothesis that he is a brain in a vat. His argument depends on a certain interpretation of EXTERNALISM. See the entry on Putnam as well as the entry TRANSCENDENTAL ARGUMENT for further discussion of Putnam's brain-in-a-vat argument.

Brentano's thesis, the thesis, due to Franz BRENTANO, that INTENTIONALITY is exhibited by all and only mental phenomena and that no physical phenomena can exhibit it. Part of Brentano's thesis, then, is the view that intentionality is the MARK OF THE MENTAL.

category mistake, due to Gilbert RYLE, especially in his book THE CONCEPT OF MIND, the mistake of treating members of distinct categories as if they belonged to the same category. Such a mistake is exhibited in an example of Ryle's, wherein a person, after visiting Oxford University and having been brought to each of the university's buildings, asks when he will be brought to the university. The category mistake committed here is thinking that a university belongs in the same category as the various buildings wherein the activities of that university take place. Ryle sought to accuse adherents of the DUALISM of DESCARTES (*see also* DUALISM, SUBSTANCE) of a category mistake. One way of characterizing what the central category mistake of Cartesian substance dualism is supposed to be is as mistakenly concluding from the fact that the mind is not a *physical entity* that it must therefore be some sort of *non-physical* entity. More accurate, at least according to Ryle, would be to conclude that the mind is no entity at all. *See also* BEHAVIORISM.

causal closure, of a set events (*see* EVENT), typically the set of all physical events, for which no member of that set is caused by events that are not members of that set. The thesis of the causal closure of the physical is the thesis that no physical events have nonphysical causes. Whatever causes they have must be physical causes. *See also* MENTAL CAUSATION; PHYSICALISM.

causal theory of content, an attempt to explain the INTENTIONALITY or CONTENT of a mental state in terms of causal relations the mental state bears to that which the mental state is about or a REPRESENTATION of. One version of the causal theory of content, closely associated with EMPIRICISM, holds that representations are the causal consequents of what they represent and that sensory PERCEPTION constitutes the essential causal link between representation and represented. Opponents of the causal theory of content allege that the theory cannot adequately account for the representation of inexistents (since causal inter-actions only obtain between things that exist), the representation of abstract entities (since causal interactions only obtain between concrete things), and the representation of the spatiotemporally remote (since causal interactions only obtain between things within certain spatiotemporal proximity to each other). *See also* CONTENT, THEORIES OF.

character, semantic (of indexicals), an aspect of the meaning of indexicals (expressions such as "I" and "now"), which remains constant across contexts, in contrast to the CONTENT of indexicals, which varies with context. For example, "now" retains a common character even when uttered at different times but has different contents at each of those times. For another example, "I" has a common character even when uttered by different people and has different contents, since it refers to the distinct people making the distinct "I" utterances.

Chinese nation, a THOUGHT EXPERIMENT and associated argument due to Ned Block, designed to cast doubt on FUNCTIONALISM and MULTIPLE REALIZABILITY. In the thought experiment, the functional roles alleged by functionalists to be definitive of mental states are occupied by Chinese citizens communicating via walkie-talkie. The number of citizens and interactions between them are imagined, in some versions, to directly correspond to the number of neurons and inter-neural interactions in a normally functioning human brain. Block alleges that the thought experiment constitutes a counterexample to FUNCTIONALISM on grounds that the Chinese nation obviously does not collectively instantiate a solitary mind (although, of course, the individual citizens each have their own minds).

An unsympathetic interpretation of the Chinese nation argument views it as an ineffectual appeal to pre-theoretic intuition: just because it is an *unintuitive consequence* of functionalism that an appropriately configured nation would give rise to a national mind, it doesn't follow that functionalism is *false*. In contrast, a sympathetic interpretation of the Chinese nation argument holds that functionalism entails that it is *impossible* for the Chinese nation to be both functionally isomorphic to a normal human and fail to give rise to a national mind. If one assumes a certain kind of connection between CONCEIVABILITY and POSSIBILITY, then, if the Chinese nation scenario as Block conceives of it is indeed conceivable, then the scenario is indeed possible.

Block's Chinese nation argument is similar in spirit and aim to John Searle's CHINESE ROOM argument. *See also* ARTIFICIAL INTELLIGENCE.

Chinese room, an argument, due to John Searle, against FUNCTIONALISM as well as certain conceptions of ARTIFICIAL INTELLIGENCE. The argument has, as a main component, the following THOUGHT EXPERIMENT: A computer program alleged by functionalists to allow a computer to conduct a conversation in Chinese is rewritten as a set of instructions in English that can be followed by John

Searle even though he understands no Chinese. Searle is imagined to sit in a room in which cards with Chinese symbols emerge from one of two slots in the wall. Searle examines each incoming card and, though comprehending no Chinese, consults instructions concerning which appropriate response card should be selected and sent out of the second of the two wall slots. The essence of the Chinese room argument against functionalism is that since Searle can follow the program without understanding Chinese, functionalism is mistaken in its contention that intelligent processes such as understanding Chinese are constituted by program-following.

One noteworthy functionalist response to the Chinese room argument has come to be known as the *systems response*. According to the systems response, it is not John Searle who is running the program, but a larger system, of which he is a mere proper part, that runs the program. This larger system includes, in addition to John Searle, the cards coming in and out of the slots, and the book that Searle consults when each new card comes in. According to the systems response, no threat is posed to functionalism by the possibility that John Searle can play his part without understanding Chinese. It is the whole system that runs the program and thus, according to the functionalist, the whole system is what understands Chinese.

Searle has countered against the systems response that the cards and the book are irrelevant and that it is possible, at least in theory, for John Searle to memorize the contents of the book (or its functional equivalent) and replace the cards with heard and spoken Chinese utterances. In this imagined scenario, John Searle hears a Chinese question and then, though he doesn't understand Chinese, consults his memory of the rule book, which describes different sounds in terms of their purely auditory, nonsemantic characteristics, and Searle then produces an appropriate sound with his mouth. Now the whole system running the program does not have John Searle as a mere proper part.

Another functionalist response to the Chinese room argument is the *robot response*. According to the robot response, the system comprising the Chinese room does not adequately satisfy the conditions for SYMBOL GROUNDING and thus no state of the system exhibits the appropriate INTENTIONALITY for understanding Chinese. If, instead, the system comprised by the whole Chinese room and its contents were embedded in a large robot so that it could act as the robot's brain, the states of the room-system could acquire intentionality in virtue of their relations to the rest of the robot and the robot's relations to its environment. Such a response emphasizes the importance of embodiment for cognition. *See* EMBODIED COGNITION.

cogito, alternately "the cogito," short for "cogito, ergo sum," attributed to René DESCARTES and oft translated as "I think. Therefore, I am." However, some controversy surrounds whether Descartes's cogito is to be regarded as an INFERENCE. One problem with regarding the cogito as an inference is that the cogito is supposed to be something that cannot be doubted and, arguably, an inference is a sequence of distinct mental states spread out in time wherein the possibility arises that as one arrives at the conclusion, one is misremembering the premises from which the conclusion is alleged to follow. On such a view of inference, it seems that if the cogito is to have the epistemic status of, for example, indubitability, it must be the sort of thing that can be present to the mind all at once. Another potential problem for the cogito is the following: Some philosophers have argued that one cannot infer the existence of a thinker from the fact of thinking but can instead only infer something like "thinking happens." *See also* SELF, THE; FIRST-PERSON AUTHORITY.

cognitive architecture, the structure of the mind. Debates over cognitive architecture concern issues such as (1) the degree to which distinct cognitive functions are realized in distinct modules (*see* MODULARITY) instead of holistically realized across multiple structural units (*see* HOLISM) and (2) whether mental states and processes are implemented as rule-governed symbol manipulations in a LANGUAGE OF THOUGHT (*see* SYMBOLICISM; GOFAI) instead of statistically associated nonsymbolic MENTAL REPRESENTATIONS (*see* CONNECTIONISM). *See also* ARTIFICIAL INTELLIGENCE; COMPOSITIONALITY; PRODUCTIVITY; SYSTEMATICITY; DYNAMIC SYSTEMS THEORY; GENERALITY CONSTRAINT.

cognitive science, the interdisciplinary study of the mind, loosely united by the idea that cognition is INFORMATION processing or COMPUTATION. Contributing disciplines include psychology, linguistics, philosophy, ARTIFICIAL INTELLIGENCE, neuroscience, and anthropology.

Cognitive science emerged in the 1970s. Many practitioners of cognitive science view themselves as rebelling against the various versions of BEHAVIORISM that dominated the previous era. In keeping with this self-conception, cognitive scientists are much more enthusiastic than behaviorists about explaining intelligent behavior by reference to MENTAL REPRESENTATION. Other topics of concern to cognitive science's practitioners are IMAGERY, PERCEPTION, MEMORY, CONCEPTS, and COGNITIVE ARCHITECTURE.

Key contributions to cognitive science include the following: In *linguistics*, CHOMSKY'S work on generative grammar. In *artificial intelligence*, the modeling of information representation by Marvin Minsky in terms of "frames." (*See* FRAME PROBLEM.) In *neuroscience*, Eric Kandel's studies of the neural mechanisms underlying the conditioning of gill retraction in the marine mollusk *aplysia*. In *psychology*, Endel Tulving's distinguishing of memory systems for semantic memory and episodic memory; Roger Shepard and Stephen Kosslyn's work on mental imagery. In *philosophy*, JERRY FODOR's elaboration and defense of the LANGUAGE OF THOUGHT hypothesis.

Among the topics that have concerned philosophers of mind interested in cognitive science have been, in addition to the topics already mentioned, topics concerning the possible REDUCTION of psychology to neuroscience and the relation of FOLK PSYCHOLOGY to scientific psychology.

color, theories of, concern issues of the nature of the colors that objects apparently have and the relation of colors to the visual experiences (*see* EXPERIENCE) by which we are aware of colors. One theory of color, *subjectivism*, is that colors are properties of visual experiences and thus not identical to any property of the physical objects that appear colored. A quite different theory, *objectivism* or *physicalism*, identifies colors with physical properties of apparently colored objects. These properties are distinct from properties of our visual experiences of color. These experiences, at least sometimes, accurately represent the objective (*see* OBJECTIVITY) colors of physical objects. Yet a third theory, *dispositionalism*, identifies colors with dispositions of physical objects to cause certain kinds of experiences in observers. *See also* PRIMARY QUALITITIES; SECONDARY QUALITIES.

compositionality, the alleged constituency of THOUGHTS out of elements common to distinct thoughts. For example, concerning the three distinct thoughts (1) *dogs sleep*, (2) *cats eat*, and (3) *dogs eat*, an advocate of the hypothesis of the compositionality of thought might say that (3) is composed of elements one of which it has in common with (1), namely, the MENTAL REPRESENTATION *dogs* and the other of which it has in common with (2), namely, the mental representation *eat*. *See also* LANGUAGE OF THOUGHT; PRODUCTIVITY; SYTEMATICITY; COG-NITIVE ARCHITECTURE; GENERALITY CONSTRAINT.

computable, of a function (*see* FUNCTION, MATHEMATICAL), the ability to have the mapping of items from the *domain* onto items in the *range* determined via an *effective procedure* (*see also* COMPUTATION). According to the Church-Turing Thesis (named after Alonzo Church and Alan TURING), a function is computable (i.e., has an effective procedure) just in case there exists a TURING MACHINE that can compute it. Functions computable by Turing machines are known as *Turing computable functions*. Though it is a minority view, some researchers have held that human beings and/or their brains are able to compute functions that are not Turing computable. This alleged noncomputability of human THOUGHT has been further alleged to constitute an obstacle to ARTIFICIAL INTELLIGENCE. *See also* GÖDEL'S INCOMPLETENESS THEOREMS.

computation, the process of arriving at a (typically numerically or symbolically interpreted) state from an initial state via the repeated application of a fixed set of operations to transform a current state into a next state; alternately, rule-governed symbol manipulation.

The definition of computation is somewhat vexed, and its historical development has been influenced by the not always congruent concerns of philosophers, mathematicians, and computer scientists. The most archaic uses of the term refer to calculation, typically of the sort done by humans solving problems involving numerically represented quantities. The notion of computation came to be associated with the notion of being effectively computable, which involves calculation via procedures that are "mechanical" in the sense of being able to be performed without the utilization of much insight or ingenuity. This notion was later developed in such a way that made it clear how the procedures in question might be *literally* mechanical—that is, performed by machines. Such notions were made mathematically precise by Alan TURING via the notion of what sorts of things can be done by a TURING MACHINE. Part of the history of these notions, and most significant for the philosophy of mind, is the hypothesis that human mental processes are themselves composed of the sorts of rule-governed and mechanistic processes distinctive of computing machines. According to some, the mind literally is a computer. *See also* ARTIFICIAL INTELLIGENCE; FUNCTIONALISM.

conceivability, the ability to be conceived. Alternately, the ability to be imagined. Characterizing conceivability in terms of IMAGINATION is somewhat problematic, since, as DESCARTES pointed out, it seems that we can conceive of things that we cannot form images of (*see* IMAGERY) as for example, conceiving as distinct a polygon with a million sides and a polygon with a million and one sides. Descartes's point aside, difficulty remains in characterizing what conceivability consists in. Controversy surrounds claims to identify conceivability with POSSIBILITY, and it is similarly controversial whether conceivability *entails* possibility. Another controversial suggestion is that conceivability be identified with the ability to be described without contradiction. For example, it is arguably inconceivable that a single object could be both red and green all over, but it is not obvious that the description "red and green all over" is contradictory in anything relevantly like the way that "red all over and not red all over" is.

concepts, mental states enabling categorization and THOUGHT. For example, one is able to categorize sparrows and robins as birds and think thoughts such as *Not all birds fly* in virtue of one's grasping or possessing of the concept of birds, or at least *a* concept of birds. The difference between having "*the* concept of birds" versus "*a* concept of birds" marks a difference between concepts regarded as publicly shareable by multiple individuals versus concepts regarded as distinctive of a particular individual. Attributing *a* concept of birds to a person leaves open the possibility that their concept of birds—the way they conceive of birds—may differ from the concepts of birds possessed by others. Attributing *the* concept of birds, in contrast, attributes something in virtue of which that person and many others besides can all be thinking about the same thing when they each think, for instance, *Birds fly*. On one construal of concepts, closely associated with the hypothesis of a LANGUAGE OF THOUGHT, concepts bear a relation to thoughts analogous to the relation that words bear to sentences.

On a very different construal of concepts from the one already discussed, concepts are not mental states, but instead nonmental abstract entities. On this latter view, when two distinct people both grasp the same concept or both possess the concept of birds, these two people are not simply in two similar mental states, they are bearing similar relations to one and the same abstract entity: the concept of birds. *See also*, CONCEPTUAL ANALYSIS; NONCONCEPTUAL CONTENT.

conceptual analysis, the process of discovering or revealing the constituents of CONCEPTS where the constituents are themselves taken to be concepts. Alternately, a conceptual analysis is the result of such a process. One hypothetical example would be the analysis of the concept of "bachelor" as "unmarried male" wherein, hypothetically, the concept of bachelorhood is hypothesized to be broken into the conceptual constituents of the concept of being a man and the concept of being unmarried.

Some philosophers have made the controversial suggestion that conceptual analysis is the primary technique for conducting philosophy. One sort of philosophical project that has attempted conceptual analysis has been the project to analyze the concept of KNOWLEDGE as *justified true belief*.

Among the various problems with the suggestion that conceptual analysis is the primary technique of philosophy or that providing analyses is one of philosophy's primary goals is the *paradox of analysis*. The paradox arises if we assume (1) that analyses should be informative, (2) that they should be synonymous with what they are analyses of, and (3) synonymous statements cannot differ in their informativeness. Consider, for instance, the proposal that the analysis of "bachelor" is "unmarried male." If "bachelor" and "unmarried male" are synonymous, then there should be no difference in meaning between "a bachelor is a bachelor" and "a bachelor is an unmarried male." However, "a bachelor is a bachelor" seems not at all informative, whereas "a bachelor is an unmarried male" is. So "a bachelor is an unmarried male," if informative, is in conflict with (2) and fails to express a synonymy and, if expressing a synonymy, is in conflict with (1) and fails to be informative.

conceptual-role semantics, (also known as "inferential-role semantics," "causal-role semantics," "computational-role semantics," and "functional-role semantics") an attempt to explain the INTENTIONALITY or CONTENT of a mental STATE in terms of relations (such as inferential relations [*see* INFERENCE]) a mental state bears to other mental states. For example, the content of my mental state concerning dogs may be constituted by relations to other mental states, such as those concerning mammals, those concerning domestication, and those concerning barking. Thus, any mental state has the content *dog* if it is a mental state that a person would be in as a result of drawing an inference from premises concerning domesticated barking mammals. Such an account of mental content seems especially compatible with the LANGUAGE OF THOUGHT hypothesis. For the same reasons that make conceptual-role semantics fit with the hypothesis of a language of thought, conceptual-role semantics is sometimes regarded as an account of the meaning of public language items. (*See also* USE THEORY OF MEANING.)

A key early proponent of conceptual-role semantics was Wilfrid SELLARS

Conceptual-role semantics is widely regarded as most plausible as an account of logical concepts and terms such as "and." Plausibly, the meaning of the truth-functional connective "and" is exhausted by the role it plays in truth-preserving inferences such as inferring from "John has slacks and Mary has a skirt" to "John has slacks." One appealing reason for extending conceptual-role semantics beyond logical items is that it promises to account for the sorts of phenomena that support the postulation of Fregean SENSE. For example, there seems to be a difference in thinking that the Morning Star is bright and that Venus is bright even though the Morning Star and Venus are one and the same astronomical body. This difference is accounted for in conceptual-role semantics by positing different conceptual roles for the MENTAL REPRESENTATION of the Morning Star and the mental representation of Venus.

Conceptual-role semantics has a certain compatibility with FUNCTIONALISM given the emphases both theories place on the *roles* played by mental states. Certain versions of conceptual-role semantics, in emphasizing relations between mental states and *de-emphasizing* relations borne to states of the external world, have been appealing to adherents of INTERNALISM and METHODOLOGICAL SOLIPSISM. Other philosophers, more impressed with the insights of EXTERNALISM, have adapted conceptual-role semantics to involve content-constituting relations to the external world in addition to relations between internal states, thus giving rise to accounts such as *two-factor conceptual-role semantics*. Many detractors of conceptual-role semantics have held that it gives rise to intolerable versions of HOLISM. *See also* CONTENT, THEORIES OF.

connectionism, a school of thought regarding ARTIFICIAL INTELLIGENCE distinguished for the modeling of cognitive processes in terms of the activities of a NEURAL NETWORK. Connectionism is sometimes viewed as a school of thought regarding COGNITIVE ARCHITECTURE that opposes both the view that cognition is rule-governed symbol manipulation (see GOFAI, SYMBOLICISM) and the LANGUAGE OF THOUGHT hypothesis. Connectionists tend instead to see cognitive processes as involving *pattern completion* and utilizing *distributed representations. See also* NEUROPHILOSOPHY; COMPUTATION.

consciousness, awareness. Alternately, the having of mental states with QUALIA. Consciousness is central to several core debates in the philosophy of mind and much contention surrounds the question of how best to define the term "consciousness" and related terms and phrases, for example, "conscious" and "conscious of." For example, for some philosophers, consciousness is equivalent to EXPERIENCE or SENSATION, while others disagree with such an equation, holding instead that there are such things as unconscious experiences or unconscious sensations. In addition to the large cluster of issues concerning the *definition* of "consciousness" are a large cluster of issues concerning the nature and possibility of an *explanation* of consciousness and related phenomena. Especially prominent have been discussions of whether consciousness will admit of any explanation consistent with either PHYSICALISM or NATURALISM.

Consciousness explained? Consciousness strikes many philosophers as something especially recalcitrant to explain (*see* HARD PROBLEM, THE). One way of putting a point on the problem is to note that it seems conceivable that two beings can be alike physically and behaviorally yet diverge with respect to WHAT IT IS LIKE for each of them to have their respective conscious states (*see* INVERTED SPECTRUM) or with respect to whether they even *have* conscious states (*see* ZOMBIE). Given the conceivability of something's being physically like me while having different or no qualia, it seems especially difficult to explain why my qualia are the way they are or even why I have any at all. Some philosophers have argued that there is a permanent EXPLANATORY GAP between conscious states and physical states and thus physicalism cannot capture the whole truth about reality. (See also the closely related KNOWLEDGE ARGUMENT.)

Consciousness defined? Some of the difficulty surrounding consciousness has to do with difficulties in defining "consciousness." Some philosophers hold that it cannot be defined, that one knows of consciousness not via grasping any defining description of it but by being directly acquainted with it in one's own case (*see* KNOWLEDGE BY ACQUAINTANCE). Other philosophers are more optimistic about whether a definition can be provided. Some urge that part of the definition will link consciousness to SELF-CONSCIOUSNESS (*see also* HIGHER-ORDER THOUGHT THEORY OF CONSCIOUSNESS). Others urge that part of the definition will link consciousness to certain kinds of MENTAL REPRESENTATION of the world. *See* FIRST-ORDER REPRESENTATIONALISM.

See also CONSCIOUSNESS, ACCESS; CONSCIOUSNESS, CREATURE; CONSCIOUSNESS, PHENOMENAL; CONSCIOUSNESS, STATE; CONSCIOUSNESS, TRANSITIVE.

consciousness, access, due to Ned Block, a term denoting a kind of CONSCIOUSNESS allegedly distinct from phenomenal consciousness (*see* CONSCIOUSNESS, PHENOMENAL), and characterized by the availability of INFORMATION in a cognitive system for the rational control of behavior and verbal report (*see* RATIONALITY; ACTION).

consciousness, creature, due to David Rosenthal, a kind of CONSCIOUSNESS attributable to an entire creature, as opposed to just a state of a creature (*see* CONSCIOUSNESS, STATE) and characterized by wakefulness, alertness, and responsiveness to stimuli.

consciousness, phenomenal, CONSCIOUSNESS characterized by there being something it's like to have it (*see* WHAT IT IS LIKE). Alternately, consciousness characterized by the presence of QUALIA. Phenomenal consciousness is alleged by Ned Block and his followers to be distinct from so-called *access consciousness* (*see* CONSCIOUSNESS, ACCESS). *See also* CONSCIOUSNESS, STATE.

consciousness, state, due to David Rosenthal, a kind of CONSCIOUSNESS attributable to a state of a creature, as opposed to a creature in its entirety. To say of a mental state, such as a DESIRE, that it is conscious (e.g., a conscious desire to drink some beer) as opposed to unconscious, is to make an attribution of state consciousness. Opinions diverge on what state consciousness consists in. One line of thought equates state consciousness with the possession by a mental state of *phenomenal properties*, also known as QUALIA. Another general approach, consistent with (but not requiring) the denial of the existence of qualia, seeks to define state consciousness in terms of transitive consciousness (*see* CONSCIOUSNESS, TRANSITIVE, which itself is defined in terms of INTENTIONALITY). One way of explaining state consciousness in terms of transitive consciousness identifies conscious states with states in virtue of which we are conscious of things in the external world. (*See also* TRANSPARENCY (OF EXPERIENCE).) Another way of explaining state consciousness in terms of transitive consciousness identifies conscious states with mental states *of* which we are conscious. (*See also* HIGHER-ORDER THOUGHT THEORY OF CONSCIOUSNESS.) *See also* UNCONSCIOUS, THE.

consciousness, transitive, being aware *of* something. Transitive consciousness is marked by there being something *of which* one is conscious, as in being conscious *of* the feeling of one's clothing. In contrast, *intransitive* consciousness involves being conscious without there necessarily being anything of which one is conscious. Many philosophers of mind see transitive consciousness as being closely related to INTENTIONALITY and MENTAL REPRESENTATION: being conscious *of* something requires having a mental representation *of* that something, as in when one has a THOUGHT *about* that something.

One controversy surrounding transitive consciousness is whether it is a requirement on state consciousness (*see* CONSCIOUSNESS, STATE). Some philosophers hold that a state is conscious only if one is conscious *of* that state. This is a view closely associated with the HIGHER-ORDER THOUGHT THEORY OF CONSCIOUSNESS. Other philosophers hold that a state can be conscious without one being conscious of that state. *See* TRANSPARENCY. *See also* CONSCIOUSNESS, CREATURE.

content, that which a REPRESENTATION is a representation of. Alternately, what an intentional mental state (a mental state with INTENTIONALITY) is about. One sort of issue concerning content that has occupied philosophers of mind has to do with what the main varieties of content are. The following three controversies are especially prominent: The first controversy concerns whether contents essentially relate subjects to the external objects and states of affairs that mental representations refer to and are true or false of (*see* CONTENT, WIDE and EXTERNALISM) or whether at least some content is constituted only by phenomena internal to the subject (*see* CONTENT, NARROW; INTERNALISM; METHODOLOGICAL SOLIPSISM). The second controversy concerns whether all content is conceptual (*see* CONCEPTS) or whether there is a kind of content, perhaps involved in PERCEPTION, that characterizes the states of even babies and nonhumans that may lack concepts (*see* NONCONCEPTUAL CONTENT). The third controversy concerns whether every content can be represented both consciously and unconsciously or whether, instead, there are contents that are distinctive of conscious states (*see* CONSCIOUSNESS). *See also* CONTENT/VEHICLE DISTINCTION; CONTENT, THEORIES OF; EXTENSION; INEXISTENCE; INTENSION (WITH AN "S"); INTENTIONALITY; REPRESENTATION, MENTAL; SEMANTICS; VEHICLE.

content, narrow, a kind of CONTENT of a mental representation (*see* REPRESENTATION, MENTAL) alleged to *not* depend on conditions external to the individual possessing the representation in question. One kind of consideration in favor of positing narrow content is the supposition that some mental representations concern things, such as unicorns, which do not exist. Some philosophers argue that it makes little sense to think of contents as external items to which one is related if the putative external item—in this case, a unicorn—does not even exist. A second kind of consideration in favor of narrow content concerns contents of concepts that don't even purport to refer to objects, such as, for instance, the content of the concept of "and." Plausibly, the content of such a concept has more to do with the role that such a concept plays in inferences (*see* INFERENCE) than with relating the concept to one or more external entities (*see* CONCEPTUAL-ROLE SEMANTICS). A third kind of consideration in favor of narrow content concerns the way in which attributing content-bearing mental states seems to involve attributing causally efficacious states in the explanation of intelligent behavior. If one assumes, however, that the causal powers of a person's states have only to do with nonrelational features of the person, then a case for narrow content seems plausible. *See* INTERNALISM. *See also* METHODOLOGICAL SOLIPSISM; INDIVIDUALISM; CONTENT, WIDE; EXTERNALISM; CONTENT, THEORIES OF.

content, theories of, concern the nature of what it is for a MENTAL REPRESENTATION to be a representation *of* something. Alternately, theories of content are theories of the nature of what it is for an intentional mental state (a mental state with INTENTIONALITY) to be *about* something. Typically, contemporary theories of content are *naturalistic* theories of content, meaning that they seek explanations of content in terms from contemporary natural science (*see* NATURALISM). However, being naturalistic is not universally agreed to be a necessary condition on theories of content, although it is one way of satisfying a requirement on noncircular explanations of intentional phenomena (the requirement that the explanations be expressible in nonintentional vocabulary). One issue of contention between different theories of content concerns whether the conditions on a representation's having content can be satisfied by conditions wholly internal to a single individual (*see* INTERNALISM; INDIVIDUALISM) or instead involve external conditions in the individual's physical or social environment (*see* EXTERNALISM). Another issue of contention between theories of content concerns whether the conditions on a representation's having content can be satisfied severally (*see* ATOMISM) or instead only in concert with other representations (*see* HOLISM). For specific theories of content, see

RESEMBLANCE THEORY OF CONTENT; ROLE THEORY OF CONTENT; CAUSAL THEORY OF CONTENT; INTENTIONAL STANCE, THE. *See also* EXTENSION; EXTERNALISM; INTENSION (WITH AN "S"); SEMANTICS; TELEOLOGY; USE THEORY OF MEANING.

content, wide, a kind of CONTENT of a MENTAL REPRESENTATION alleged to depend on conditions external to the individual possessing the representation in question. See EXTERNALISM. *See also* CONTENT, NARROW; INTERNALISM; CONTENT, THEORIES OF.

content/vehicle distinction, the difference between what a representation is a representation *of* (CONTENT) and the representation *itself*. The vehicle is that which *has* the content. The content/vehicle distinction may be usefully compared to an analogous distinction that applies to linguistic items: the distinction between *use* and *mention*. In the sentence "There are only six letters in 'Boston' and more than six people in Boston," the first instance of "Boston," appearing in quotation marks, is *mentioned*, not *used*, whereas the second instance is *used*, not *mentioned*. Mentioning the word calls attention to features of the word itself, not what the word names. Similarly, we can alternately call attention to features of a mental state independently of what the mental state might represent. Consider that I remember today what I ate yesterday. Occurring today is a feature of the MEMORY itself—a fact about the memory's vehicle—whereas occurring yesterday is a feature of what I remember—a fact about the memory's content.

de dicto, Latin for "of what is said," contrasted against *de re*, Latin for "of the thing." There are several distinctions that philosophers have drawn in terms of *de dicto* and *de re*, but perhaps most important to philosophers of mind is an apparent distinction between two kinds of belief or two kinds of belief-ascription. Consider, for illustration, what would have to be true about Jones and his surroundings in order for the following sentences to be true:

1. Jones believes that Smith's favorite song is playing.
2. Jones believes of Smith's favorite song that it is playing.

There is a relatively natural reading of (2) whereby it can be true regardless of whether Jones is of the opinion that the song playing is indeed Smith's favorite song. Suppose, as a matter of fact, both that Smith's favorite song is "Born to Run" and that Jones has no idea that "Born to Run" is beloved by Smith. Perhaps Jones conceives of that song under some description or other, such as "as the song by Bruce Springsteen once proposed to be adopted as the state song of New Jersey," but does not conceive of the song under the description "the song most favored by Smith." We may read (2) as being consistent with all of the following:

3. Jones believes that "Born to Run" is playing.
4. Smith's favorite song is "Born to Run."
5. Jones does not believe that "Born to Run" is Smith's favorite song.

To read (2) in such a way is to read it as attributing a *de re* belief to Jones.

In contrast, we may read (1) in such a way that if (1) and (3) were both true, (5) would have to be false, on pain of Jones holding contradictory beliefs. To read (1) in such a way is to read it as attributing a *de dicto* belief to Jones. *See also* INTENSIONALITY.

de re, see DE DICTO.

de se, Latin for "of oneself." If I have a BELIEF about myself as such, that is, if I believe that *I* am the author of this book (as distinct from my believing that *Pete Mandik* is the author of this book) I therefore have a *de se* belief.

desire, an appetitive PROPOSITIONAL ATTITUDE. An attitude of wanting a PROPOSITION to be true. For any proposition P, *a desire that P* is an attitude that, in concert with a BELIEF concerning some proposition Q, would constitute, at least partially, a REASON for and cause of someone's ACTION to bring about P. For example, George is opening the refrigerator because he desires that (P) he drinks some beer and he believes that (Q) there is a bottle of beer in the refrigerator. Desires may be contrasted with beliefs in terms of their differing DIRECTION OF FIT: The aim of belief is to have contents (*see* CONTENT) that match the world, whereas the aim of a desire is to have the world modified in such a way as to satisfy the desire. *See also* FOLK PSYCHOLOGY; INTENTIONAL STANCE; INTENTIONALITY; REASONS.

direct realism, a theory of PERCEPTION that holds, in opposition to IDEALISM and PHENOMENALISM, that *what* we perceive—the *object of perception*—exists independently of our perceiving it and, in opposition to REPRESENTATIVE REALISM aka INDIRECT REALISM, that *how* we perceive is *not* via an either conscious or unconscious INFERENCE that begins with the direct awareness of a MENTAL REPRESENTATION and ends by hypothesizing the existence of a mind-independent entity. Also known as "naïve realism," direct realism has the appealing feature of capturing the commonsense supposition that perception is a direct, unmediated relation to a real object. One of the main challenges raised against direct realism is that of accounting for an apparent similarity between accurate perceptions of real objects on the one hand and, on the other hand, hallucinations, dreams, and illusory perceptions. To illustrate the challenge, if a hallucination of an elephant can be subjectively indistinguishable (i.e., indistinguishable from the FIRST-PERSON point of view) from the accurate perception of an elephant, and it makes sense to posit a mental-representational object of AWARENESS in the hallucination case, it seems inviting to posit a mental-representational object for the accurate perceptual case as well—an object that serves as an intermediary between the perceiver and the real elephant. This line of thought is the main component of the ARGUMENT FROM ILLUSION. One sort of response available to the direct realist is to deny that the two sorts of situations really can be subjectively indistinguishable.

direct reference, the theory that the meaning of a term or the CONTENT of a MENTAL REPRESENTATION is simply its *extension* (see EXTENSION (1)). In its purest form, the theory of direct reference does not posit the existence of SENSE as one of the components of meaning or content.

direction of fit, of a mental state, a characteristic concerning whether the world is supposed to match it or it is supposed to match the world. BELIEF exhibits world-to-mind direction of fit: The aim of belief is to have contents (*see* CONTENT) that match the world. In contrast, desire exhibits mind-to-world direction of fit: The aim of desire is to have the world modified in such a way as to satisfy desire. A contrast of direction of fit applies as well to certain speech acts. For instance, *assertions* have world-to-mind direction of fit and *commands* have mind-to-world direction of fit. G.E.M. Anscombe illustrated this sort of contrast in terms of two otherwise identical lists: one a shopper's shopping list, the other a list generated by a private investigator tailing the shopper and noting the items bought.

disembodiment, the state of lacking a body after previously having one. While the possibility of disembodiment is embraced by various religious thinkers as part of a doctrine of the immortality of the soul, it is inconsistent with most versions of PHYSICALISM.

disjunction problem, a problem that arises for theories of CONTENT (*see also* CONTENT, THEORIES OF), especially versions of the CAUSAL THEORY OF CONTENT, which involves providing an EXPLANATION of why a MENTAL REPRESENTATION has, as its content, something like, for example, *cow* instead of *cow-or-horse*, given that mental representations of that TYPE may be caused by not just cows but by either cows or horses. Another way of conveying what the problem is involves focusing on mental representations as they figure in PERCEPTION and asking what factors, *other than* causal factors, are to distinguish accurate perceptual representations of cows as cows from inaccurate representations of cows as horses given that there are conditions in which a cow can cause one to (accurately) represent it as a cow (veridical perception) and conditions in which a cow can cause one to (inaccurately) represent it as a horse (misperception).

doxastic, of, or pertaining to, BELIEF. *See also* SUBDOXASTIC.

dualism, a general position concerning the MIND/BODY PROBLEM wherein both the existence and distinctness of mental and physical entities (properties or substances) is affirmed (*see* PROPERTY; SUBSTANCE). *See also* DUALISM, PROPERTY; DUALISM, SUBSTANCE.

dualism, property, a kind of DUALISM, consistent with monism about substances (*see* SUBSTANCE), wherein mental properties (*see* PROPERTY) are regarded as distinct from and irreducible to physical properties (*see* REDUCTION). One family of considerations in favor of property dualism hinges specifically on QUALIA (*see* EXPLANATORY GAP; KNOWLEDGE ARGUMENT). Another consideration in favor of property dualism hinges on a certain interpretation of MULTIPLE REALIZABILITY: If a mental property is multiply realizable by physical properties in such a way that there are two distinct realizations that have no physical properties in common, then there is no common physical property that the multiply realized mental property can be identical to and thus the mental property must be distinct from *all* physical properties. *See also* ANOMALOUS MONISM; PHYSICALISM, NONREDUCTIVE; TOKEN-IDENTITY THESIS; SUPERVENIENCE.

dualism, substance, a kind of DUALISM wherein both minds and physical bodies are affirmed to exist and it is further affirmed that their existence is distinct in the sense that each can exist without the other. In contrast with property dualism (*see* DUALISM, PROPERTY), substance dualism is the view that minds and physical bodies are distinct things or substances, each of which are not properties but may *have* properties. It may further be affirmed that there are distinct properties that each kind of thing may have. For instance, it may be held by a substance dualist that only physical bodies may have spatial properties such as shape and location (*see* EXTENSION (2)) and only minds may have properties such as RATIONALITY, INTENTIONALITY, or QUALIA.

Substance dualism was famously argued for by DESCARTES. According to Descartes, key distinguishing features of minds and physical bodies were that he knew for certain that his mind existed (*see* COGITO; RES COGITANS) and he did not know for certain that any physical bodies existed (*see* RES EXTENSA).

duck-rabbit, an ambiguous figure or drawing interpretable as looking like either the head of a rabbit or the head of a duck. Some philosophers and psychologists have used the existence of such ambiguous figures to argue that the nature of PERCEPTION is underdetermined by either SENSATION or the INFORMATION transduced by the sensory receptors. *See* UNDERDETERMINATION, PERCEPTUAL.

dynamic systems theory, a branch of mathematics describing the behavior of complex systems in terms of differential equations. Dynamic systems theory has been promoted by some philosophers of mind and cognitive scientists (*see* COGNITIVE SCIENCE) as a way of thinking about COGNITIVE ARCHITECTURE that is distinct from both SYMBOLICISM and CONNECTIONISM. *See also* EMBODIED COGNITION.

eliminative materialism, a kind of PHYSICALISM or MATERIALISM that denies the existence of anything mental. Less extreme forms of eliminative materialism deny the existence of only a limited number of mental entities, as in the denial of the existence of the sorts of mental entities posited by FOLK PSYCHOLOGY, (see BELIEF; DESIRE), where such a denial is consistent with the positing of non-folk-theoretic mental entities, such as those posited in CONNECTIONISM. See also NEUROPHILOSOPHY.

eliminativism, ELIMINATIVE MATERIALISM.

embodied cognition, a research program in COGNITIVE SCIENCE that emphasizes the importance of a creature's real-time ("online" instead of "offline") sensory-motor engagement with its environment. Such a research program thus deemphasizes the sorts of offline planning, REASONING, and problem-solving processes that were central explanatory targets of classical approaches of ARTIFICIAL INTELLIGENCE and SYMBOLICISM. Some embodied-cognition researchers view COGNITION as emerging (see EMERGENCE) from organism-environment interactions. See also EMBODIMENT; DYNAMIC SYSTEMS THEORY; EXTENDED MIND.

embodiment, the having of a body in sensory-motor contact with an environment, especially as it contributes to the nature of one's own PHENOMENOLOGY. In addition to being emphasized in certain works of phenomenology, embodiment is a central concept in the EMBODIED COGNITION approach to COGNITIVE SCIENCE.

emergence, the arising of a PROPERTY in a relatively unpredictable way from the interaction of other properties. Alternately, the INSTANTIATION of a property by a whole that is due to "more than the sum of its parts," or, less colloquially, due to properties of the parts in a way more complicated than mere summing. Part of what's difficult in supplying a viable notion of emergence is the task of characterizing a relevant notion of unpredictability that isn't due simply to the current ignorance of investigators. Early proponents of the existence of emergent properties claimed that certain chemical properties such as the liquidity or solubility of certain chemical samples were emergent on the grounds that they could not be predicted by KNOWLEDGE of the nature and interaction of their atomic constituents. However, as chemistry and physics progressed, such claims were discovered to be false. Another difficulty in supplying a viable notion of emergence is in giving a precise meaning to the imprecise phrase "more than the sum of its parts." We can see that there are clear cases in which the property of a whole is more than a sum of properties of its parts but that the properties of the whole are unlikely to be regarded by anyone as having *emerged* from the properties of the parts. For example, the temperature of a gas is the average kinetic energy of its constituent molecules. As such, it is thus not simply the sum of the kinetic energy of each of the molecules. It is instead the sum of their kinetic energy *divided* by the number of molecules. There's a sense in which being a divided sum of its parts is more than the sum of its parts: Since it involves division, it involves a further arithmetical operation than mere summing. However, this seems not to get at the sort of thing that emergentists have had in mind, perhaps since the result of the operation is insufficiently surprising or unpredictable. Emergentism, the proposal that there exist emergent properties, is closely related to nonreductive physicalism (*see* PHYSICALISM, NONREDUCTIVE). Emergence has also played a relatively significant role in recent work within the EMBODIED COGNITION approach to COGNITIVE SCIENCE, where some researchers have proposed that COGNITION is an emergent feature of organism-environment interactions.

emotion, an affective mental state, examples of which include states of fear, anger, disgust, and joy. Emotions are often regarded as obstacles to RATIONALITY, but they play central roles in quality of life, personal preferences and priorities, social affiliations, and morality. Emotions may be distinguished from other mental states such as judgment or BELIEF by the relative closeness of association between emotions and characteristic bodily reactions (e.g., increased heart rate, perspiration). Emotions may be differentiated from one another along numerous dimensions such as (1) the presence and type of INTENTIONAL OBJECT (*see* INTENTIONALITY), (2) intensity, and (3) valence (positive versus negative). So, for an example concerning (1), joy and resentment may be distinguished by what they are about or directed at, where resentment is directed toward other people in a way that joy need not be. For an example concerning (2), irritation and rage may be distinguished by, among other things, their intensity. For an example concerning (3), joy and fear have opposite valences, with there being a relatively obvious sense in which one is more positive than the other.

empiricism, traditional empiricism may be defined by the slogan that *there is nothing in the mind that is not first in the senses* and defined less sloganistically as the view that all knowledge is justified only by sensory perception and we can meaningfully conceive of only what we can perceive (or at least imagine perceiving) with our senses. Traditional empiricism is opposed to RATIONALISM. More recently, empiricism has come to be associated with the view in the philosophy of science that affirms the existence of only observable entities and thus denies the existence of unobservable theoretical posits (*see also* PHENOMENALISM).

epiphenomenalism, the view of mental states and mental properties, especially QUALIA, that they have no effects (though they may themselves *be* effects). For examples of arguments for epiphenomenalism, *see* EXPLANATORY EXCLUSION and KNOWLEDGE ARGUMENT. *See also* INTERACTIONISM.

epistemology, a major branch of philosophy concerned with the investigation of KNOWLEDGE and related topics, including PERCEPTION, MEMORY, BELIEF, and TRUTH. One major area of overlap between epistemology and the philosophy of mind is the problem of other minds (*see* OTHER MINDS, PROBLEM OF). *See also* VERIFICATIONISM; COGITO; EMPIRICISM; RATIONALISM; SKEPTICAL HYPOTHESIS; TRANSCENDENTAL IDEALISM.

event, something that happens. One prominent philosophical view of events, due to Jaegwon KIM, defines an event as the INSTANTIATION of a PROPERTY by an object at a time. A contrasting view, due to Donald DAVIDSON, views events as particulars that are primitive (and thus, for example, not reducible to objects, properties, and times) and enter into causal relations. For Davidson, one and the same event may be subsumed under either a mental description or a physical description and will enter into causal relations regardless of which way it is described.

evolutionary psychology, a research program within psychology that seeks to explain aspects of human COGNITION by construing those aspects as survival-conducive adaptations developed through biological evolution. One popular idea among evolutionary psychologists is that the mind consists of multiple single-purpose modules (*see* MODULARITY).

experience, an occurrent mental state, typically sensory and conscious, that serves as input to mental processes such as MEMORY, REASONING, and the formation of BELIEF. In philosophy of mind, "experience" is often modified by "conscious," as in "conscious experience," although it is a matter of contro-versy whether there are nonconscious experiences (*see* BLINDSIGHT) and is modified by "sensory," as in "sensory experience," although it is a matter of controversy whether there are nonsensory experiences. *See also* CONSCIOUSNESS; PERCEPTION; SENSATION.

explanation, something that aids in the understanding of something else (or, in the cases that are self-explanatory, something that aids in the under-standing of itself). Alternately, explanation is the act or process of providing such an understanding. A useful terminological contrast for philosophers discussing explanation is to distinguish *explanandum* and *explanans*. The explanandum is what is explained, whereas the explanans is what does the explaining—the explanation itself. In the classical model of explanation—the *deductive-nomological model of explanation*—an EVENT is explained when a description of its occurrence is logically derived from a set of statements, at least one of which is a statement of NATURAL LAW.

One prominent issue in the philosophy of mind concerning explanation has to do with the question of whether folk-psychological (*see* FOLK PSYCHOLOGY) explanations of human ACTION in terms of REASONS are significantly distinct from the explanations of physical events in terms of causes. Some philoso-phers, following DAVIDSON, view *causal* explanations of physical events, but not *rationalizing* explanations of human action, as involving appeals to natural law.

Another prominent issue in the philosophy of mind concerning explanation has to do with the question of whether the sorts of explanations consistent with PHYSICALISM must necessarily leave something out about mentality, espe-cially QUALIA (*see* EXPLANATORY GAP). *See also* EXPLANATORY EXCLUSION.

explanatory exclusion, a problem that arises for MENTAL CAUSATION given certain common assumptions of PHYSICALISM—namely that (1) every physical EVENT has a physical cause (*see* CAUSAL CLOSURE) and (2) for every mental event there is a physical event that suffices for it (a physical event that is the REALIZA-TION of the mental event and upon which the mental event supervenes [*see* SUPERVENIENCE]). The problem that arises is in seeing how it can be consistent with (1) and (2) to make the commonsense assumption, (3): that mental events are causes—that is, that they have effects. For any alleged effect E of a mental event M, there should be, by (1), a physical event P that is the cause of E. It is likely, given (2), that P is the physical realization or supervenience base of M. If P suffices for E, then there looks to be no work for M to do. P suffices to explain E and thus excludes M from counting as an explanation of E. Such considerations may be utilized to argue for EPIPHENOMENALISM. *See also* EXPLANATION.

explanatory gap, a gap alleged to arise between any proposed physicalist (*see* PHYSICALISM) EXPLANATION of consciousness (*see*, especially, CONSCIOUSNESS, PHENOMENAL; QUALIA) and consciousness itself. The idea of such an explanatory gap can be mobilized in an argument against physicalism. One way of representing such an explanatory-gap argument against physicalism is as having the following premises: Premise One, If physicalism is true, then consciousness can be wholly explained in terms of physical entities and processes. Premise Two, Consciousness cannot be wholly explained in terms of physical entities and processes. The crucial premise, Premise Two, is alleged to be true because for any set of physical entities and processes proposed to suffice for consciousness, it will always be an open question *why* they suffice for consciousness. Like the KNOWLEDGE ARGUMENT and the MODAL ARGUMENT, the explanatory-gap argument is an *epistemic-gap* argument against physicalism. All three arguments infer from a gap between the physical and the phenomenal that arises concerning what we can know, explain, or conceive (an epistemic gap), a corresponding gap in ONTOLOGY between physical properties (*see* PROPERTY) and phenomenal properties. *See also* HARD PROBLEM, THE.

extended mind, the hypothesis that mental states themselves, as opposed to the factors determining their CONTENT, extend beyond the physical boundaries of an organism to include environmental phenomena. The extended-mind hypothesis may thus be characterized as a kind of *vehicle* EXTERNALISM and contrasted against *content* externalism (*see* VEHICLE; CONTENT/VEHICLE DISTINCTION). A key argument for the extended-mind hypothesis advanced by Andy Clark and David CHALMERS involves a THOUGHT EXPERIMENT concerning two characters, Inga and Otto (their names are evocative of "inner" and "outer"), who both make their way to a museum they've been to previously. Otto's "memory" of where the museum is located is not encoded in his nervous system (he's imagined to be an Alzheimer's patient with difficulty doing such a thing) but is instead written down in his notebook. Inga, however, has no external record of the location of the museum but remembers the location in the usual way of what we would consider her MEMORY, perhaps by accessing INFORMATION stored in her nervous system. Clark and Chalmers urge the conclusion that the distributed system that includes Otto's brain and notebook counts as no less a SUPERVENIENCE base for a (vehicle of) BELIEF than does Inga's purely (or, at least, more) internal system.

extension (1), in SEMANTICS, the set of entities of which a predicate is true. Two predicates that differ in their INTENSION (WITH AN "S") or SENSE may nonetheless be coextensive—that is, have the same extension. For example, "chordate" ("creature with a heart") and "renate" ("creature with kidneys") share their extension in spite of not sharing their intension. More broadly, the notion of extension may be applied to linguistic items other than predicates. For example, the extension of a name or referring expression is the entity named or referred to. Gottlob Frege held that the extension of an entire sentence was its truth-value. Thus, two true sentences would both have the same extension.

extension (2), in the substance dualism (*see* DUALISM, SUBSTANCE) of René DESCARTES, the possession of spatial magnitudes and properties (e.g., size, shape, and motion) by a SUBSTANCE. *See also* RES EXTENSA; PRIMARY QUALITIES.

externalism, the view of the mental states of an individual that they (the mental states) may have as their physical SUPERVENIENCE bases something of greater spatiotemporal extent than the individual himself or herself. Alternately, any view that holds that either mental states themselves or the factors determinative of a state's CONTENT extend beyond the physical boundaries (skull and skin) of the individual who possesses the mental states. This latter construal of externalism allows us to sort externalistic theories into two sorts: VEHICLE externalism and content externalism (*see* CONTENT/VEHICLE DISTINCTION). Another way of sorting externalistic theories, a way that cuts across the content-externalism vs. vehicle-externalism division, sorts externalistic theories in terms of whether they apply to QUALIA (*see* CONSCIOUSNESS, PHENOMENAL) or instead only to nonphenomenal aspects of the mind—for example, allegedly nonphenomenal intentional states such as beliefs (*see* BELIEF). The four kinds of externalism generated by these two cross-classifying distinctions (content-vehicle, intentional-phenomenal) may be usefully labeled as follows: (1) intentional-content externalism, (2) intentional-vehicle externalism, (3) phenomenal-content externalism, and (4) phenomenal-vehicle externalism.

Intentional-content externalism is probably the most discussed in the litera-ture. One version of it may be described as follows: Individuals who have the same intrinsic physical properties may nonetheless diverge in the content of the thoughts they express when they say "This is water" if the substance called "water" in their respective environments is chemically distinct (H_2O in the one and XYZ in the other). Content that depends on external factors is often referred to as "WIDE CONTENT." (*See* SWAMP MAN; TWIN EARTH; XYZ.)

One version of intentional vehicle externalism has been defended by Andy Clark and David CHALMERS under the heading of the "extended-mind hypothesis" (*see* EXTENDED MIND).

Contemporary defenders of phenomenal-content externalism, such as Michael Tye and Fred DRETSKE, identify qualia with the contents of certain kinds of MENTAL REPRESENTATION and then are led to externalistic conclusions via an embrace of an externalistic theory of content, such as a version of the CAUSAL THEORY OF CONTENT or TELEOSEMANTICS. Such phenomenal content externalists also embrace FIRST-ORDER REPRESENTATIONALISM about CONSCIOUSNESS as well as the thesis that experience is transparent (*see* TRANSPARENCY (OF EXPERIENCE)).

Phenomenal-vehicle externalism is perhaps the least popular of the four kinds of externalism so far. But it does have advocates, notably Alva Noë and Susan Hurley. Advocates of this approach frequently emphasize the role of EMBODIMENT in structuring our PHENOMENOLOGY.

See also INTERNALISM.

family resemblance, a set of similarities that may hold between various items subsumed under a concept (*see* CONCEPTS) even though there is no single set of conditions that all of the items share. That many concepts do not admit of analyses into necessary and sufficient conditions (*see* CONCEPTUAL ANALYSIS) but instead apply to items that are related by a loose collection of family resemblances was a point famously emphasized by Ludwig WITTGENSTEIN in his *Philosophical Investigations*. Wittgenstein's key illustration of family resemblance involved all the multifarious things that may be regarded as *games*, some of which can be won (e.g., chess), some of which cannot (e.g., a game of catch), some of which require multiple players (e.g., baseball), and some of which require only one (e.g., solitaire). The psychologist Elenor Rosch's *prototype theory* of concepts and categorization applies Wittgenstein's family-resemblance idea to concepts in general. Wittgenstein's remarks on family resemblance, especially as applied to the concept of games, was challenged by the philosopher Bernard Suits in his 1978 book *The Grasshopper: Games, Life and Utopia*. Suits offers a definition of playing a game, a succinct version of which is "the voluntary attempt to overcome unnecessary obstacles."

first-order representationalism, a theory of CONSCIOUSNESS that explains state consciousness (*see* CONSCIOUSNESS, STATE) in terms of having a certain kind of MENTAL REPRESENTATION (crucially, a representation that need not be represented by any other representation, thus "first-order") and explains QUALIA or the "WHAT IT IS LIKE" aspects of consciousness (*see* CONSCIOUSNESS, PHENOMENAL) in terms of the CONTENT of the relevant mental representation. The main distinctive feature of first-order representationalism is that unlike higher-order representationalisms, such as the HIGHER-ORDER THOUGHT THEORY OF CONSCIOUSNESS or the higher-order PERCEPTION theory of consciousness, it does not make it a requirement on a state's being conscious that it be represented by itself or any other state. One consideration that first-order representationalists raise in support of this part of their view is that it appears, or so it is claimed, that we cannot become aware of the features of an EXPERIENCE itself as opposed to features of what the experience is an experience *of*. For example, when I attend to my experience of a blue rectangle, it seems that I am only aware of the blueness and the rectangularity—properties presumably instantiated not by my experience but by some physical object in the external world: a blue rectangle. *See* TRANSPARENCY (OF EXPERIENCE).

first-person, a point of view alleged to involve special access to special facts, where what is special is characterized as subjective and private—a point of view contrasted against the objective and public "third-person view" or "view from nowhere." In ordinary language, English text written in the first person uses INDEXICAL words such as "I" and "me" to refer to the author of that text. If the author refers to himself or herself by the use of his or her own name, then the text thereby produced is written in the third person. (When "you" is utilized in reference to you, the reader, the text is written in the second person.) Analogous remarks apply to spoken English. Some philosophers of mind have elevated the contrast between the first and third person into a contrast between subjective and objective kinds of knowledge and, even more strongly, a contrast between two realms of things known. Many have claimed that each of us enjoys a special FIRST-PERSON AUTHORITY with respect to our own mental states. *See also* OBJECTIVITY; SUBJECTIVITY.

first-person authority, the allegedly superior level of warrant or justification one has with respect to one's own mental states, especially as mediated via the faculty of INTROSPECTION. (*See also* FIRST-PERSON.) The degree and scope of first-person authority has been subjected to much criticism in contemporary philosophy of mind. Claims of first-person authority can be seen as attributing three distinct epistemological properties (*see* EPISTEMOLOGY) to the deliverances of introspection—INFALLIBILITY, INCORRIGIBILITY, and transparency (*see* TRANSPARENCY (OF THE MIND TO ITSELF)—each of which may be subjected to separate criticisms.

The claim of *infallibility* is the claim that if one has a BELIEF that one is in such-and-such mental state, then that belief must be true. The claim of *incorrigibility* is that even if a belief about one's own mental state is false, no one *else* can be in a position to correct one about this. The claim of *transparency,* sometimes described as a claim that one's own mental states are *self-intimating*, is the claim that if something is happening in one's own mind, then one must have a true belief about it.

One kind of consideration in favor of infallibility is the COGITO of René DESCARTES. Another consideration in favor of infallibility (for at least a restricted class of mental states) is that some mental states are themselves a form of APPEARANCE and, as such, do not admit of a distinction between appearance and reality that would be required for one to be wrong about them. One kind of consideration against infallibility, and which can also serve as a source of considerations against transparency, is the hypothesis of the existence of the unconscious (*see* UNCONSCIOUS, THE), popularized by Sigmund Freud and his followers, which contains many beliefs and desires (*see* DESIRE) of which one may have no AWARENESS (thus contradicting transparency) or, in repression or denial, one may come to have false beliefs about them, thus undermining infallibility. A related kind of consideration against infallibility and transparency comes from studies of BLINDSIGHT wherein certain neuropsychological patients lack true beliefs about their own visual EXPERIENCE.

Against incorrigibility, some philosophers have presented arguments based on a THOUGHT EXPERIMENT concerning the employment of a "super-cerebroscope" by a scientist who claims that a patient is having a green experience even while the patient falsely believes of himself that he is having a red experience. If the super-cerebroscope scenario is possible, then one does not have incorrigible access to such mental states.

folk psychology, the commonsense understanding of mental phenomena wherein the behavior of humans and some other animals is predicted and explained (*see* EXPLANATION) in terms of BELIEF and DESIRE as the REASONS for ACTION. Controversy surrounds the question of whether this understanding is constituted by a *theory* believed by the folk (*see* "THEORY"-THEORY (THEORY OF MIND)). Some philosophers have argued that if folk psychology is constituted by a theory, then it is evaluable in accordance with the standards applicable to scientific theories. One branch of this line of thought holds that folk psychology fares quite poorly when measured by such standards and thus should be dismissed in favor of some kind of ELIMINATIVE MATERIALISM. Some advocates of eliminative materialism hold that talk of belief and desire should be eliminated in favor of predictions and explanations of human behavior in neuroscientific terms (*see* NEUROPHILOSOPHY). One way of opposing this line of thought is by denying that we attribute beliefs and desires to one another by applying a theory, but instead understand the mental states of others by simulating them using our own mental states (*see* SIMULATION THEORY (THEORY OF MIND)). *See also* THEORY OF MIND; INTENTIONAL STANCE, THE.

frame problem, the problem, originating in ARTIFICIAL INTELLIGENCE research, of creating a system that is capable of drawing correct inferences (*see* INFERENCE) about a changing world given all the ways in which things *don't change* in a given situation. For example, while *people* do not have difficulty in realizing that an object painted blue and then moved into another room will still be blue after the change in location, an *artificial intelligence* (AI) that is *explicitly* programmed to have KNOWLEDGE of all of the relevant changes (e.g., changing location) and nonchanges (e.g., not changing color) that have to do with moving an object to another room would have to be programmed to know an *indefinite* number of nonchanges (e.g., moved objects generally don't explode, moved objects generally don't change size). However, providing an AI with an indefinitely large set of "frame axioms" concerning relevant nonchanges is not a feasible programming feat. Researchers have explored solutions to the frame problem that involve utilizing different formats of knowledge representation (e.g., IMAGERY) and different principles of inference (e.g., nonmonotonic logic).

free will, minimally, the alleged faculty in virtue of which a person is able to act as he or she wants. (*See* ACTION.) Some philosophers make an additional claim about such a faculty, namely that the relevant action be in *no way* caused (or, more broadly, in no way determined). Without this additional claim, the existence of free will is compatible with the determination, causal or otherwise, of human action. With the addition, free will and the determination of action are incompatible. One sort of reason that philosophers hold human action to be determined has to do with ideas closely associated with PHYSICALISM, ideas such as CAUSAL CLOSURE: If every EVENT has a physical cause and all physical causation is governed by NATURAL LAW, it seems that everything that *does* happen happens *by necessity. See also* WILL, THE; INTENTION.

function, mathematical, a relation between two sets, the *domain* of the function and the *range* of the function, such that each element, x, in the domain is associated with exactly one element, y, in the range (though it is left open whether there are many elements in the domain associated with each element in the range). Mathematical functions, especially COMPUTABLE mathematical functions, have played key roles in discussions of COMPUTATION and ARTIFICIAL INTELLIGENCE.

function, teleological, the notion of function most closely related to TELEOLOGY is that of the *purpose, aim,* or *goal* of something like a mental state, bodily trait, or behavior. Alternately, what something is *for*. Many philosophers are interested in the grounding of teleological function. One account that applies especially well to the teleological function of artifacts is that what something is for (what its function is) is largely determined by the INTENTION of the artifact's designer. However, for those philosophers who reject the existence of God or any other supernatural designer, such an analysis may not be suitable when applied to things, such as the traits and behaviors of naturally occurring organisms, that are not artifacts. Alternate accounts seek to ground teleological function in terms of evolution by natural selection. On one version of this sort of account, the teleological function of a trait or behavior is the survival-enhancing effect that such a trait or behavior has had on the ancestors from whom it was inherited and explains (partially) *why* it was inherited. For example, the function of my heart is to pump blood, because pumping blood promoted the survival of my ancestors and explains (partially) why I inherited a heart from my ancestors. One aspect of teleological function that has attracted philosophers of mind is its INTENSIONALITY (*see also* INTENSION (WITH AN "S")). For example, an eye can *have* the function of seeing even though it fails to *perform* the function of seeing (as in the eye of a blind person). Some philosophers of mind have been attracted to the possibility of explaining the intensionality of mental states (as in a BELIEF in or a DESIRE for a nonexistent state of affairs) by reference to the intensionality of teleological functions. *See* TELEOSEMANTICS.

functionalism, the view that what is essential to a mental state's being what it is, is what *role* it plays in a functional and/or causal economy that relates it to the sensory inputs, motor outputs, and other mental states of the entity possessing the mental state in question. This characterization of what *is* essential here leaves open an oft-discussed possibility of what is *not* essential to a mental state's being what it is—namely what particular constitution, material or otherwise, serves to *realize* (*see* REALIZATION) the role the mental state plays. This characterization thus leaves open whether mental states might be multiply realizable (*see* MULTIPLE REALIZABILITY). While most functionalists subscribe to PHYSICALISM and thus hold that all realizers of the functional roles definitive of mental states must be *physical* realizers, it is consistent with functionalism to embrace DUALISM and thus hold that mental states have nonphysical realizers.

generality constraint, due to Gareth Evans, a constraint on the possession of CONCEPTS, according to which a subject is able to possess a concept only if the subject is capable of applying the concept to multiple things and is capable of applying other concepts to those same things. Alternately, the generality constraint may be expressed as a constraint on THOUGHT such that a subject is only able to think a thought of the form *X is F* if the subject is also able to think of things other than *X* that they, too, are *F* and to think of *X* something besides the fact that it is *F*—for instance, that it is *G*. Evans's generality constraint is a descendent of a thesis defended by P. F. Strawson in discussing the problem of other minds (*see* OTHER MINDS, PROBLEM OF). Strawson argued that one could not conceive of oneself as being in PAIN without also being capable of conceiving of others as being in pain. *See also* SYSTEMATICITY.

ghost in the machine, due to Gilbert RYLE in THE CONCEPT OF MIND, a description of the relation of the mind (the "ghost") and body (the "machine") as conceived of by DESCARTES's substance dualism (*see* DUALISM, SUBSTANCE), a view of which Ryle was highly critical.

given, that which is known noninferentially in virtue of having a sensory PERCEPTION, as opposed to that which is known via an INFERENCE on the basis of a sensory perception. In other words, that which perceptual EXPERIENCE *grants* as opposed to what is *figured out* on the basis of perceptual experience. To illustrate, upon sticking my finger in some hot water and feeling it to be hot, I may, on the basis of that experience, plus prior KNOWLEDGE, come to infer that the water's constituent molecules have a high average kinetic energy, but my AWARENESS of the *hotness* is alleged to not be the result of any inference, but is just immediately present to my mind in virtue of having this experience (*see* KNOWLEDGE BY ACQUAINTANCE). Some philosophers have held that what's given in perception can serve as a foundation for all other knowledge. That there is such a given in perception was famously criticized by Wilfrid SELLARS (*see* GIVEN, MYTH OF THE). *See also* NONCONCEPTUAL CONTENT.

given, myth of the, the doctrine, held by Wilfrid SELLARS to be mistaken, that there are states of knowers, typically conceived of as states of SENSATION or PERCEPTION, that can obtain without the acquisition (via learning) by the knower of any CONCEPTS or any abilities to draw any kind of INFERENCE, yet may nonetheless serve as the justification of KNOWLEDGE. Sellars held, in opposition to the doctrine of given-ness, that no states of subjects could serve as justifications for knowledge or REASONS for BELIEF without the subject possessing, at the time of having knowledge, various acquired concepts and inferential abilities. *See also* GIVEN; EMPIRICISM. *See also* NONCONCEPTUAL CONTENT.

Gödel's incompleteness theorems, a set of theorems proven by the Austrian logician Kurt Gödel in 1931. The main idea of what Gödel demonstrated can be conveyed relatively informally, as follows: For any formal system sufficiently powerful to express the truths of arithmetic, there exists a true sentence—that system's *Gödel sentence*—which is expressible in the language of that system but is not provable within that system. Some researchers, notably Jon Lucas and Roger Penrose, have tried to base criticisms of ARTIFICIAL INTELLIGENCE upon Gödel's results. The strength of such criticisms hinge on the controversial premise that a human mind is able to grasp the truth of its own Gödel sentence. *See also* COMPUTABLE; COMPUTATION.

GOFAI (Good Old-Fashioned Artificial Intelligence), coined by John Haugeland to refer to certain approaches to ARTIFICIAL INTELLIGENCE and related views of COGNITIVE ARCHITECTURE. Also referred to as SYMBOLICISM.

group mind, a hypothetical mind, aka a "hive mind," that depends on members of a group such that it is not the mind of any one of the members of the group. The individual members of the group may either be individually mindless or individually in possession of minds distinct from the group mind.

hard problem, the, the problem (largely associated with David CHALMERS, who popularized this usage of "hard problem" in the philosophy of mind), of explaining QUALIA or phenomenal consciousness (*see* CONSCIOUSNESS, PHENOMENAL). *See also*, EXPLANATORY GAP.

higher-order-thought theory of consciousness, an approach to explaining state consciousness (*see* CONSCIOUSNESS, STATE) and phenomenal consciousness (*see* CONSCIOUSNESS, PHENOMENAL) whereby a state is conscious if one is conscious *of* the state (*see* CONSCIOUSNESS, TRANSITIVE) by having a THOUGHT about the state. WHAT IT IS LIKE to be in a conscious state is explained, on some versions at least, in terms of how that state is represented by a higher-order thought. Thus, for example, my state of PERCEPTION becomes a conscious state in virtue of my having a higher-order thought to the effect that I am in such a state of perception. Further, if how I think of the perception is as being a perception of a red object, then *what it is like* for me at that moment is like perceiving a red object. According to some adherents of the higher-order-thought theory of consciousness, the thought in question must satisfy further requirements such as being arrived at by some means other than as a consequence of a conscious INFERENCE. Such further requirements are added since it seems highly implausible that just any thought about one of my mental states should suffice to make that state conscious. Suppose, for instance, I infer, on the basis of adherence to principles of Freudian psychology, that I have certain unconscious beliefs and desires. My thinking about those beliefs and desires in such a case seems not to suffice to thereby render them conscious.

holism, the thesis, contrasted with ATOMISM and closely related to CONCEPTUAL-ROLE SEMANTICS, that mental states have their CONTENT largely if not wholly in virtue of their relations to other mental states. One sort of consideration in favor of holism is that it seems inconceivable that a thinker should be able to have just a single THOUGHT or just a single BELIEF. For example, it seems inconceivable that there could be a being capable of entertaining only the thought that *Some dogs have thick fur* without being able to think any other thought about dogs, fur, or thickness or think any other thought of the form *Some blankity-blanks are such-and-such*. Related to such a concern, *see* SYSTEMATICITY and GENERALITY CONSTRAINT. One sort of consideration *against* holism is a consideration raised against versions of holism whereby if any two thinkers differ in *any* of their beliefs, then they must differ in *all* of their beliefs. For example, if two thinkers have differing beliefs about dogs, say one believes that a dog once ate her sandwich and the other doesn't believe this, then, if the nature of a person's belief is determined by *all* of the other beliefs a person has, then these two thinkers can't be thinking the same thing when they each think a thought they would express by saying "Some dogs have thick fur." One way of protecting holism from such a consequence is to draw a distinction between, for a given belief, the other beliefs that help determine its content and the other beliefs that do not. However, this strategy for protecting holism seems to resurrect a version of the analytic/synthetic distinction against which W.V.O. QUINE presented highly influential criticisms.

homunculus, Latin for "little man," the term is used by some philosophers to ridicule certain positions as positing the existence of a homunculus inside of a person to explain how that person accomplishes some psychological function. For instance, an explanation that explains a person's ability to see in virtue of the creation of mental images that are apprehended with the "mind's eye" seems prone to the charge of positing a homunculus or committing a "homuncular fallacy." The problem here is that the alleged explanation threatens an infinite regress. If a person's ability to see something is explained by some inner faculty or homunculus that itself perceives something, the question arises of how that inner entity is able to perceive anything. (*See* INDIRECT REALISM.) Is some additional homunculus, a homunculus within a homunculus, to be posited? Some philosophers, notably Daniel DENNETT, have embraced as virtuous certain forms of "homuncular" explanation: explanations regarded as virtuous as long as each successive homunculus in a nesting series of homunculi is stupider than the one before it and the entire series bottoms out in entirely unintelligent mechanisms. This view is a kind of FUNCTIONALISM labeled "homuncular functionalism."

idealism, in its global form, a kind of MONISM whereby everything is ultimately mental and so-called physical bodies have no existence independent of, for example, someone's perceptions of or ideas about them (*see also* PHENOMENALISM). In its various local forms, idealism involves affirming the mind-dependence of some restricted domain of entities. Thus, we may interpret as local idealisms the views that nothing is good or bad but thinking makes it so or that beauty is in the eye of the beholder. *See also* SECONDARY QUALITIES.

identity theory, also known as type-identity theory (*see* TYPE) and reductive physicalism (*see* PHYSICALISM, REDUCTIVE), the view that all mental types or properties are identical to some physical types or properties (*see* PROPERTY). For example, it is the hypothesis that the mental type PAIN is identical to the physical or neurophysiological type *c-fibers firing*. The label "type-identity theory" serves to demarcate this thesis from one known as "token-identity theory," the latter of which is consistent with nonreductive physicalism (*see* PHYSICALISM, NONREDUCTIVE) and involves affirming that while no mental type is identical to any physical type, every mental TOKEN is identical to some physical token. The token-identity theorist's opposition to type-identity theory may be seen as analogous to the view that while no color is identical to any shape, every colored object is also a shaped object.

imagery, mental states that share a format with states of sensory PERCEPTION and not states of THOUGHT and share with thoughts and not perceptions the possibility of endogenous triggering. Imagery is not exclusively visual. That is, in addition to visual images, there may also be tactile, auditory, olfactory, and gustatory states of imagery. Just as one may imagine seeing a rose's color, so may one imagine smelling its fragrance. One sort of controversy surrounding imagery is whether mental images are best accounted for by an appeal to a RESEMBLANCE THEORY OF CONTENT whereby mental images literally resemble that which they are images of. Literal pictures resemble that which they are pictures of, but controversy surrounds whether a similar point is true of "mental pictures." One sort of worry about a resemblance account of mental imagery is that it confuses the *plausible* resemblance between imagining and seeing a rose with an *implausible* resemblance between an imagining of a rose and the rose itself. Another sort of worry about the resemblance account is whether it applies to mental imagery in all sensory modalities—that is, to olfactory imagery, auditory imagery, etc. While some supporters of the resemblance account appeal to evidence that the brain areas implicated in *visual* imagery involve the utilization of literal geometrical similarities between patterns of activity in the brain and visual shapes of imagined objects, there's no support and little plausibility to the claim, for instance, that the brain processes involved in olfactory imagery literally smell like the fragrances of which they are images. *See also* IMAGINATION.

imagination, the faculty by which one is able to have mental IMAGERY. Alternately, and more broadly, the faculty in virtue of which one may entertain nonactual as well as actual possibilities in ways not limited to imagery (*see* POSSIBILITY). In this latter sense of "imagination," discussions of imagination are closely tied to discussions of issues surrounding CONCEIVABILITY.

immediacy, being present to the mind but not in virtue of any mediating STATE or entity. According to DIRECT REALISM, the objects of PERCEPTION (physical objects, which are perceived) are present to the mind without any mediating AWARENESS of a MENTAL REPRESENTATION (as in INDIRECT REALISM aka REPRESENTATIVE REALISM). On some versions of the thesis of KNOWLEDGE BY ACQUAINTANCE, things that are known, namely SENSE-DATA or QUALIA, are present to the mind immediately. *See also* DIRECT REFERENCE.

impression, *see* SENSATION.

incorrigibility, distinct from an inability to be *wrong* (*see* INFALLIBILITY), instead, the inability to be *corrected* by anyone else. It is sometimes held that beliefs about one's own mental states, especially beliefs about one's own current mental states or beliefs formed via the faculty of INTROSPECTION are incorrigible. Claims of incorrigibility with respect to one's own mental states are often made in conjunction with, although they are distinct from, claims of INFALLIBILITY and transparency (*see* TRANSPARENCY (OF THE MIND TO ITSELF)). *See also* FIRST-PERSON AUTHORITY.

indeterminacy of translation, the thesis defended by W.V.O. QUINE that for any given language, there will always be multiple alternate ways of translating that language that are equally well supported by all the evidence that could possibly be available to a translator. Quine developed his case for this thesis via the contemplation of a THOUGHT EXPERIMENT concerning RADICAL TRANSLATION—an attempt to translate an unfamiliar language into a familiar one without recourse to bilingual speakers. One famous illustration of Quine's involved a radical translator confronted with the question of whether utterances of "gavagai" in the presence of rabbits should be translated into English as "rabbit" or instead as "un-detached rabbit part." Since every presentation of a rabbit is also the presentation of an un-detached rabbit part, it is exceedingly difficult to see how any amount of evidence could favor one of the translations of "gavagai" over another. *See also* INSCRUTABILITY OF REFERENCE.

indexical, a linguistic or mental item TYPE, tokens of which have a distinct CONTENT depending on the distinct contexts of their tokenings (*see* TOKEN; TYPE-TOKEN DISTINCTION). Examples include "I," which refers to different individuals when spoken by different individuals, and "here" and "now," which respectively refer to different places and times when spoken at different places and times. *See also* DE SE; CHARACTER, SEMANTIC (OF INDEXICALS).

indirect realism, *see* REPRESENTATIVE REALISM. *See also* DIRECT REALISM.

individualism, the view of the mental states of an individual that they (the mental states) may have as their physical SUPERVENIENCE bases properties only of the individual himself or herself. Individualism is closely associated with INTERNALISM, the latter of which is contrasted with EXTERNALISM. The label "individualism" serves to contrast internalism against versions of externalism that put heavy emphasis on *social* factors (such as the presence of experts in the community) in the determination of the CONTENT of mental states.

inexistence, simple nonexistence, in some uses, but in other uses, the peculiar ontological status of the objects of intentional states (*see* INTENTIONALITY) such that they, the "objects," need not have actual existence but nonetheless, in some sense, "exist." *See also* SUBSISTENCE.

infallibility, an inability to be wrong. More specifically, an inability to have a BELIEF and have it be false. It is sometimes held that beliefs about one's own mental states, especially beliefs about one's own current mental states or beliefs formed via the faculty of INTROSPECTION are infallible. Claims of infallibility with respect to one's own mental states are often made in conjunction with, although they are distinct from, claims of INCORRIGIBILITY and transparency (*see* TRANSPARENCY (OF THE MIND TO ITSELF). *See also* FIRST-PERSON AUTHORITY.

inference, a sequence of mental states whereby one reasons (*see* REASONING) and arrives at a conclusion from one or more premises. Alternately, the mental ACTION whereby one arrives at a conclusion from one or more premises.

information, a property of a state or event, X (a signal), enabling one to infer (*see* INFERENCE) truths about some state or event Y (where X and Y are usually distinct). For example, a ringing doorbell is a signal, the hearing of which puts the listener in a position to infer that someone is at the door. Alternately, "information" may be used to refer to the truths about Y that X enables inferences of. For example, the information carried by a ringing doorbell may be the following truth: Someone is at the door. The mathematical theory of information (Shannon and Weaver's "Mathematical Theory of Communication") provides means for defining *amounts* of information (such as "bits") in terms of the number and probability of possible events. Philosophical theories of information strive to define the semantic CONTENT of information— that is, they strive to define not *how much* information a signal carries but instead *what* information a signal carries. Various philosophical conceptions of information define signal content in terms of what events are either causally, nomologically, or probabilistically correlated with the occurrence of a signal. The notion of information may be utilized to characterize various mental states, such as states of PERCEPTION and MEMORY, as information-bearing states—states by which a creature respectively acquires and retains information about its environment. The notion of information has also been used by some philosophers as a basis for understanding INTENTIONALITY and CONTENT (*see* INFORMATIONAL THEORY OF CONTENT). A further use of information of significance for the philosophy of mind is in characterizations of COMPUTATION as "information processing."

informational theory of content, an attempt to explain the INTENTIONALITY or CONTENT of a mental state in terms of what that state is either causally, nomologically, or probabilistically correlated with. For example, the content of my mental state concerning dogs may be constituted by causal relations that state bears to dogs (such as, if my eyes are open and I'm in a well-lighted room with a dog, then I'll be caused to go into that state). The informational theory of content is closely related to the CAUSAL THEORY OF CONTENT. Such theories of content are appealing to some philosophers of mind because of the apparent consistency of such theories with ATOMISM. Such consistency may be seen to derive from the fact that, in defining the content of mental representations of dogs in virtue of relations to dogs and not in virtue of relations to other mental representations, the informational theory of content is thus consistent with the denial of HOLISM that is central to atomism. Jerry FODOR is a prominent proponent of both atomism and the informational theory of content. *See also* CONTENT, THEORIES OF.

innateness, the property, of either a trait or a capacity, of being inborn, unlearned, or unacquired, especially as applies to KNOWLEDGE, CONCEPTS, ideas, and abilities. Conflicts over which aspects of the mind, if any, are innate are characteristic of the divide between EMPIRICISM and RATIONALISM, with empiricists being comparatively less likely to view any mental phenomenon as being innate. Noam CHOMSKY famously defended the view that much of the knowledge required for speaking and understanding language is innate.

inscrutability of reference, a version of W.V.O. QUINE's thesis of the INDETERMINACY OF TRANSLATION as applied specifically to items of language involved in REFERENCE. Thus, for example, while there may be some indeterminacy involved in translating sentences such as "The rabbit is cute" and "Mandik writes" as being true, the inscrutability of reference has specifically to do with referring expressions and terms such as "the rabbit" and "Mandik."

instantiation, of a PROPERTY, there being a particular having the property, where it is a particular instance of the property. For example, a red shoe and a red car are distinct particulars, each of which *has* the property of redness and each of which count's as *instances* of red things. The shoe and the car each *instantiate* the property of being red. The notion of instantiation plays a crucial role in various discussions in the philosophy of mind. Controversies over PHYSICALISM and SUPERVENIENCE in the philosophy of mind may be cast as controversies over whether the instantiation of mental properties requires the instantiation of physical properties. Controversies over MULTIPLE REALIZABILITY may be cast as controversies over whether distinct instances of mental properties can differ with respect to which physical properties are instantiated. Certain issues surrounding INTENTIONALITY and INEXISTENCE concern whether one can have a BELIEF or a THOUGHT about properties that have no instances (such as the property of being a unicorn).

instrumentalism, a view of the ontological status of the entities posited by scientific theories whereby they are held to lack objective existence but to be nonetheless useful to talk about as if they existed. Positing their existence is held to be a *mere* aid in calculation and prediction, an aid that does not thereby commit the scientist to their real existence. In the philosophy of mind, Daniel DENNETT'S INTENTIONAL STANCE account of PROPOSITIONAL ATTITUDES has been interpreted as a form of instrumentalism. *See also* REALISM.

intelligence, the possession of the capacity for THOUGHT and REASONING. *See also*, ARTIFICIAL INTELLIGENCE; TURING TEST.

intension (with an "s"), in SEMANTICS, the aspects of significance other than extension (*see* EXTENSION (1)). Such aspects of significance are exemplified by predicates and referring expressions that share extension yet differ in their intension or SENSE. One possible way of understanding intension is in terms of inferential roles or conceptual roles, whereby predicates that are coextensive may nonetheless play different roles defined by differing sets of relations to other predicates. (*See also* CONCEPTUAL-ROLE SEMANTICS.) On another kind of understanding of intensions, they are a certain kind of abstract object, where the extension of a name may be the concrete particular thereby named or the intension of a name may be an abstract object, a "sense," or "mode of presentation." One way of applying the extension/intension distinction to whole sentences is to identify the extension of a sentence with a truth value (true or false) and identify the intension of a sentence with a PROPOSITION. *See also* INTENSIONALITY.

intensional fallacy, an invalid argument for the distinctness of entities based on mistaking intensional differences for extensional ones (*see* INTENSIONALITY; INTENSION (WITH AN "S"); EXTENSION (1)). To illustrate what's fallacious about the intensional fallacy, consider that while Lex Luthor may believe that Superman is bulletproof and believe that Clark Kent is vulnerable to death by gunshot, it would be fallacious to conclude that Superman and Clark Kent are two different people from this difference, since this difference is merely a difference in Lex Luthor's beliefs, not any difference between the entity referred to as "Superman" and the entity referred to as "Clark Kent." On one interpretation of Descartes's argument for the distinctness of the mind from any physical body, the argument runs as follows: My mind has the property of being known for certain to exist (*see* COGITO). No physical body has the property of being known for certain to exist (*see* SKEPTICAL HYPOTHESIS). Therefore, my mind is not identical to any physical body (including my brain). If this argument is committing the intensional fallacy, then the allegedly different properties had by my mind and my body are more like the differences in Lex Luthor's beliefs than any real difference between Clark Kent and Superman. It may not be a genuine property that my mind has and my brain lacks that I know it under the description "thing that exists for certain." Some philosophers, notably Paul CHURCHLAND, have charged certain versions of the KNOWLEDGE ARGUMENT against physicalism of committing the intensional fallacy. *See also* LEIBNIZ'S LAW.

intensionality, aka "opacity" (*see* OPACITY, REFERENTIAL), failure of extensionality—that is, the failure, in certain contexts, so-called opaque or intensional contexts, to be able to substitute co-referring terms without changing the truth value of the larger context. For example, quotation exhibits intensionality in the following manner: The true sentence *John wrote "Mark Twain had a mustache" on the board*, would be rendered false if "Samuel Clemens" were substituted for "Mark Twain" even though the names "Samuel Clemens" and "Mark Twain" are co-referring—that is, they both name one and the same individual. In contrast, the true sentence, "John is the same height as Mark Twain," would remain true with a substitution of "Samuel Clemens" for "Mark Twain." Examples of intensional contexts aside from quotation include attributions of mental states and statements about modality (necessity, possibility, etc.). For an example concerning mental-state attribution, it may very well be true that John believes that Mark Twain has a mustache but not that John believes that Samuel Clemens has a mustache. Some philosophers hold that while DE DICTO beliefs may give rise to this sort of intensionality, DE RE beliefs do not. An example of a de re belief attribution would be to say that John believes *of* Mark Twain that he has a mustache. John may also be said to believe *of* Samuel Clemens that he has a mustache, even though John does not have the de dicto belief *that* Samuel Clemens has a mustache (since John may not realize that Mark Twain and Samuel Clemens are one and the same individual). Though intensionality (spelled with an "s") is closely related to INTENTIONALITY (spelled with a "t"), it is worth noting that not all instances of intensionality have to do with intentionality. For example, consider intensional contexts having to do with modality. Such examples include "Necessarily, two is less than five," which may be true and rendered false by substituting "five" with the co-referring expression "the number of fingers on Mandik's left hand." It is possible, although hopefully it doesn't ever happen, that the number of fingers on my left hand becomes less than five.

Another key feature of intensionality is its failure to support existential generalization. For example, one cannot infer from "John believes that Santa Claus is fat" that there exists an entity such that John believes it to be fat. In contrast, one can infer from "John is standing next to the flagpole" that there exists something such that John is standing next to it. *See also* INEXISTENCE.

intention, a feature of ACTION as in when one *intentionally* (as opposed to unintentionally) sticks one's foot out to trip someone. Alternately, a kind of mental STATE, an *intention*, which is directed toward an action—often some possible future action.

One approach some philosophers have taken to supply an account of intention as a feature of action is to give an account of *intentional* actions whereby they are the sorts of behaviors the EXPLANATION of which cites REASONS. On one such account, then, intentional actions are those that are explicable by reference to the BELIEF and DESIRE of an AGENT. So, for example, John's drinking beer counts as an intentional drinking of beer if he has certain desires, certain beliefs about how to satisfy those desires, and the drinking of the beer is a certain kind of causal consequence of John's beliefs and desires.

One kind of account of what it means for there to be a mental state, which is an intention—as in, an intention to perform some action at some future date—relates intention as a mental state to the above account of intentional action. On one such account, John's intention to drink beer at the end of the week is a belief that John has that bears certain relations to other beliefs as well as desires that John has. On other sorts of accounts, an intention is a sort of mental state distinct from belief and desire. *See also* WILL, THE; WEAKNESS OF WILL.

intentional action, *see* INTENTION.

intentional object, of a mental state that has INTENTIONALITY or *aboutness*, that which the mental state is about. For example, if one has a BELIEF that Santa

Claus will deliver presents on Christmas Eve, then the intentional object of the belief is Santa Claus. One peculiar feature of intentional objects is their INEXISTENCE: as in the case of Santa Claus, the intentional object of a mental state need not actually exist.

intentional stance, the, due to Daniel DENNETT, the viewpoint from which one is in a position to explain (*see* EXPLANATION) the behaviors of a system by attributing to it states with INTENTIONALITY (such as BELIEF and DESIRE) and viewing its behaviors as conforming in varying degrees to the norms (*see* NORMATIVE) of RATIONALITY. Dennett contrasts the intentional stance with both the *physical stance* and the *design stance*. The physical stance involves explaining behaviors only in terms appropriate for the objects of the physical sciences (physics, chemistry, etc.). The design stance involves explaining behaviors in terms of what purposes (*see* FUNCTION, TELEOLOGICAL) they may serve and is appropriate for explaining the behaviors of artifacts as well as the products of evolution by natural selection (*see* TELEOLOGY). Dennett has seemed to intend the intentional stance as useful in accounting for what it is for something to have intentionality: Something's having intentionality is just something's being usefully predictable or explicable when viewed from the intentional stance. Some philosophers have been critical of such a view of intentionality as insufficiently consistent with REALISM about intentional states. *See also* SCIENTIFIC REALISM; FOLK PSYCHOLOGY; THEORY OF MIND.

intentionality, the directedness of the mind upon its objects; the *aboutness* of mental states that are about something; the possession, by mental states, of CONTENT; the relating, or quasi-relating, of a mental state such as a BELIEF or a DESIRE toward its INTENTIONAL OBJECT. Some controversy surrounds the question of whether nonmental entities such as words and pictures may have intentionality and, if so, whether nonmental instances of intentionality are derivative phenomena, with the only instances of nonderivative, original intentionality being mental instances. The remainder of this entry will focus on the intentionality of mental states.

The philosophical notion of intentionality originates primarily from the medieval era and was introduced into contemporary philosophical discussions via the work of Franz BRENTANO. Brentano held intentionality to be the MARK OF THE MENTAL and to pose a permanent obstacle to PHYSICALISM or MATERIALISM.

One especially problematic feature of intentionality, the feature that makes it especially difficult to regard it as a physical phenomenon, is the INEXISTENCE of intentional objects. One way of highlighting the problem of intentional inexistence is via the contemplation of the following inconsistent triad concerning an intentional state such as a THOUGHT.

1. To have a thought about something is to bear a relation to a thing that is thereby thought about.
2. One can bear relations only to things that exist.
3. One can have thoughts about things that do not exist.

Each of the three items in this triad is independently plausible, but taken together, it is clear that they cannot all be true. Different philosophers have held varying positions about intentionality that involve rejecting one or more of the items in the inconsistent triad.

One key feature of intentionality (with a "t") is its relation to INTENSIONALITY (with an "s"). This may be brought out with respect to item (3) in the inconsistent triad: Another way of highlighting the intensionality of intentional states is in terms of DE DICTO belief: John may believe that Mark Twain had a mustache and believe that Samuel Clemens did not have a mustache even though "Mark Twain" and "Samuel Clemens" are names for one and the same person.

Another key feature of intentionality is that intentional mental states may be characterized in terms of their DIRECTION OF FIT. For example, a belief is supposed to be true of aspects of the world, but a desire is not supposed to conform to the way the world is. Instead, the world has to be a certain way in order for the desire to be satisfied.

One sort of question that arises is whether *all* mental states have intentionality. Another sort of question that arises is whether the mental properties of states include *only* their intentionality. Call these the "all" and "only" questions, respectively. Regarding the "all" question, philosophers have wondered whether intentionality is a property of mental states other than the paradigmatically intentional examples of belief, desire, PERCEPTION, and INTENTION. To what degree, if at all, does intentionality attach, for instance, to states of EMOTION or SENSATION? Regarding the "only" question, philosophers have wondered whether phenomenal characteristics or QUALIA should be regarded as mental properties that are distinct from intentionality. One sort of position to hold with respect to both the "all" and the "only" question, is to hold that, for instance, a sensation of PAIN has *no* intentionality. On this position, pain doesn't, for example, represent any part of the world as being any particular way, and the mental properties of this state are exhausted by qualia such as phenomenal intensity and negative valence. An opposing position, such as that held by some adherents of FIRST-ORDER REPRESENTATIONALISM, is that a sensation of pain does have intentionality, that the intentional object of a sensation of pain is some part of the body, and that the sensation represents the tissue in that body part as being disturbed or damaged. Thus, on such a view, a sensation of pain has a direction of fit similar to a belief or a state of perception. *See also* CONTENT, THEORIES OF.

interactionism, the view that mental events may have physical effects and that physical events may have mental effects. Interactionism is thus opposed to both EPIPHENOMENALISM and OCCASIONALISM. *See also* MENTAL CAUSATION.

internalism, the view of the mental states of an individual that they (the mental states) may not have, as their physical SUPERVENIENCE bases, anything of greater spatiotemporal extent than the individual himself or herself. According to internalism, then, individuals who are physically intrinsically similar will not differ mentally even though they may differ in terms of extrinsic physical properties. Internalism is opposed to EXTERNALISM. While internalism is arguably implicit in many traditional philosophical views, explicit defenses of internalism largely emerged only in reaction against various externalist positions that began to be defended in the latter parts of the twentieth century.

Another way of characterizing internalism is as being any view that holds that either mental states themselves, or the factors determinative of the CONTENT of mental states, do not extend beyond the physical boundaries (skull and skin) of the individual who possesses the mental states. This latter construal of internalism allows us to sort internalist theories into two categories: VEHICLE internalism and content internalism (*see* CONTENT/VEHICLE DISTINCTION). Another way of categorizng internalist theories—a way that cuts across the content-internalism vs. vehicle-internalism division—sorts internalist theories in terms of whether they apply to QUALIA (*see* CONSCIOUSNESS, PHENOMENAL) or instead to only nonphenomenal aspects of the mind, for example, allegedly nonphenomenal intentional states such as beliefs (*see* BELIEF). The four kinds of internalism generated by these two cross-classifying distinctions (content/vehicle, intentional/phenomenal) may be usefully labeled as follows: (1) intentional-content internalism, (2) intentional-vehicle internalism, (3) phenomenal-content internalism, and (4) phenomenal-vehicle internalism. These four kinds of internalism may be understood in opposition to the four correlative external-ist positions. For further discussion of the four kinds of position, see the entry on EXTERNALISM.

Intentional-content internalism is probably the most discussed in the litera-ture. One version of it may be described as follows: Individuals who have the same intrinsic physical properties may not diverge in the CONTENT of the thoughts they express when they say "This is water" even if the substance called "water" in their respective environments is chemically distinct (H_2O in the one and XYZ in the other). Content that depends only on internal factors is often referred to as "NARROW CONTENT." (See SWAMP MAN; TWIN EARTH; XYZ.)

See also INDIVIDUALISM.

introspection, the faculty by which the mind is known to itself without the KNOWLEDGE in question being the consequence of an INFERENCE. Introspection shares with PERCEPTION the feature of being a means to noninferential knowl-edge, but differs from perception in providing noninferential knowledge about the *mind*. Despite this key difference between introspection and perception, some philosophers hold that introspection is sufficiently similar to perception to be regarded as a faculty of *inner-sense*. Against the view that introspection is a kind of perceptual faculty is the following consideration: In the sensory perception of, for instance, a red square, there arises a sensory intermediary between my AWARENESS of the square as red and the red square itself. This intermediary is a SENSATION, in this case a sensation of redness (and perhaps also a sensation of squareness). The presence of a sensation is what makes this awareness a *sensory perception* as opposed to a mere THOUGHT or BELIEF that a red square is present. By analogy, if introspection is sensory as opposed to merely a kind of thought or belief, then it would be natural to suppose that when introspecting a sensation itself, there should be an additional intermediary, this time a sensation of the sensation. However, many philosophers find it an implausible suggestion that there are such higher-order sensations—that is, sensations of sensations. A different kind of position to hold about the introspection of perceptual states is that not only does introspection fail to reveal any sensations of sensations (higher-order sensations), but we are incapable of being introspectively aware of even first-order sensations. For more on this view, *see* TRANSPARENCY (OF EXPERIENCE).

Another set of controversies surrounding introspection involve those outlined in the entry on FIRST-PERSON AUTHORITY concerning whether introspective beliefs have an epistemological status (*see* EPISTEMOLOGY) or level of justification superior to nonintrospective beliefs.

intuition, a means by which propositions appear (*see* APPEARANCE) to the mind to be true (or false), a means allegedly distinct from means such as PERCEPTION, MEMORY, INFERENCE, and testimony. Alternately, instead of a noninferential, nonperceptual, etc. means by which propositions *appear* to be true, a noninferential, nonperceptual, etc. means by which propositions are *known* to be true. Much controversy surrounds the claim that there is such a separate means of knowledge. Nonetheless, that certain propositions are intuitively true is something that many philosophers regard as a constraint on philosophical theorizing. A recent philosophical movement known as *experimental philosophy* involves employing the empirical techniques from the social and psychological sciences to survey the intuitions of various people regarding various philosophical topics. *See also* CONCEPTUAL ANALYSIS, THOUGHT EXPERIMENT.

inverted spectrum, a hypothetical scenario wherein a person is systematically different with respect to their QUALIA relative to someone else despite the fact that the two people are behaviorally, functionally, and/or physically similar. Such an example would be if two people equally proficient at sorting paint chips and calling the colors by their correct names nonetheless differed in that where the one person had red qualia in response to red chips and green qualia in response to green chips, the other person had red qualia in response to green chips and green qualia in response to red chips. The inverted-spectrum hypothesis has been mobilized in various arguments against PHYSICALISM, FUNCTIONALISM, and BEHAVIORISM. To sketch one example, if two numerically distinct beings can be physically similar (i.e., share all of their intrinsic physical properties) but inverted with respect to their qualia, then qualia cannot be identical to any intrinsic physical properties. *See also*, MODAL ARGUMENT.

know-how, procedural KNOWLEDGE. Knowledge, the possession of which thereby enables one to be able to do something. Controversy surrounds the question of whether know-how or knowing-how is distinct from propositional knowledge (knowing-that). Gilbert RYLE, in his THE CONCEPT OF MIND, emphasized the distinctiveness of know-how and criticized what he called "intellectualist" accounts of intelligent ACTION. According to Ryle, the intellectualist is committed to the view that every intelligently performed act is the consequence of some mental episode of deliberation. However, as Ryle pointed out, deliberation is something that can be done either well or poorly—that is, either intelligently or unintelligently. Positing yet another state of deliberation to explain the intelligence of the first state looks to lead straightforwardly to an infinite regress. Ryle's solution to breaking the regress was to emphasize an analysis of intelligence in terms of know-how conceived of as a kind of disposition.

Another area in the philosophy of mind where know-how, conceived of as distinct from more "intellectualist" conceptions of knowing, has played a prominent role is in certain discussions of the KNOWLEDGE ARGUMENT against physicalism. Some physicalists have argued that the knowledge argument fallaciously treats knowledge of WHAT IT'S LIKE as a kind of propositional knowledge instead of a kind of knowing-how. According to this "ability hypothesis" response to the knowledge argument, knowing what it's like to see red is to have an ability to imagine and recognize red things, as opposed to knowing the TRUTH of some PROPOSITION about QUALIA.

knowledge, justified true BELIEF. There has been much philosophical discussion of whether this analysis is adequate for *all* kinds of knowledge as well as whether it is adequate for *any* kinds of knowledge. Against its adequacy for *all* kinds of knowledge, it has been suggested, for example, that perhaps KNOW-HOW is a kind of knowledge that can be had without thereby having a justified true belief. (*See also* KNOWLEDGE BY ACQUAINTANCE.) Against its adequacy for *any* kind of knowledge, one of the most famous lines of opposition involves a class of counterexamples associated with Edmund Gettier wherein one has a justified true belief that such-and-such is the case but fails to thereby *know* that such-and-such is the case.

knowledge argument, an argument against PHYSICALISM due to Frank Jackson wherein the key premises concern claims to the effect that a person may know all of the physical facts without thereby knowing WHAT IT IS LIKE to have an EXPERIENCE with such-and-such QUALIA (*see also* CONSCIOUSNESS, PHENOMENAL). An oft-discussed THOUGHT EXPERIMENT that supports or illustrates the central claim of the argument involves a futuristic super-neuroscientist, Mary, who knows all of the physical facts concerning the neural basis of human color vision but has not herself ever seen the color red. Many philosophers have found it intuitive to suppose that despite being *physically* omniscient she learns something new when she finally gets around to seeing something red. If the KNOWLEDGE gained is factual or propositional, then an antiphysicalist conclusion naturally follows. If Mary already knew *all* of the physical facts and learns an additional fact, this additional fact must be a *nonphysical* fact.

One of the general sorts of ways in which physicalists have questioned the cogency of the knowledge argument has been by questioning whether, instead of factual knowledge, knowledge of what it is like to have qualia is constituted by, for example, a kind of KNOW-HOW or, alternately, a kind of KNOWLEDGE BY ACQUAINTANCE. Like the EXPLANATORY GAP argument and the MODAL ARGUMENT, the knowledge argument is an *epistemic-gap* argument against physicalism. All three arguments infer from a gap between the physical and the phenomenal that arises concerning what we can know, explain, or conceive (an epistemic gap), to a gap in ONTOLOGY between physical properties and phenomenal properties.

knowledge by acquaintance, a kind of KNOWLEDGE alleged to be distinct from other kinds of knowledge (such as knowing *that* some proposition is true or knowing *how* to do some task) in that it requires a special sort of relation between the knower and what is known. Bertrand Russell postulated such a kind of knowledge wherein the relation to what is known is a relation of *direct* AWARENESS that is to be contrasted against a mediated or indirect knowledge *by description*. Russell held additionally that while we could know our own mental states by the direct relation of acquaintance, our knowledge of physical objects was indirect. *See also* DIRECT REALISM; DIRECT REFERENCE.

language of thought, a hypothesis, most closely associated in the contemporary literature with Jerry FODOR, that the medium wherein THOUGHT and REASONING take place is constituted by a system of combinable symbols (*see* SYMBOLICISM)—a system that bears significant similarities to written and spoken languages (though it is often held to be MENTALESE, a language distinct from languages such as English and French). The language-of-thought hypothesis is a version of the *representational theory of the mind*, for it explains one's being in a mental state like having a thought or a BELIEF in terms of one's bearing a relation to a MENTAL REPRESENTATION. The language-of-thought hypothesis is distinct from other versions of the representational theory of mind for its emphasis on the nature of mental representation being language-like and its denial that mental representation is either picture-like (*see* IMAGERY) or of the distributed nature posited by advocates of CONNECTIONISM.

One kind of advantage of positing language-like mental representations is that it helps to explain how, unlike representations such as pictures, thoughts can be *generic*. For example, one can think *There are some dogs in the yard* without thinking of a specific number of dogs. In contrast, a picture of some dogs in the yard will picture some specific number of dogs. For another example, one can think *There is an extremely large dog in the yard* without having any thought as to what color the dog is. It is exceedingly difficult, in contrast, to obtain a picture of a dog's being extremely large that isn't also a picture of a dog's being some specific color.

Explaining the generic nature of thought is not the only virtue pointed out by adherents of the language-of-thought hypothesis. The language-of-thought hypothesis is additionally supposed to explain the SYSTEMATICITY and PRODUCTIVITY of thought. A crucial aspect of the explanation is the hypothesis of COMPOSITIONALITY.

Leibniz's law, the identity of indiscernibles. Alternately, the conjunction of both the identity of indiscernibles and the indiscernibility of identicals. The thesis of the identity of indiscernibles is this: If x and y are to have all and only the same properties in common, then x and y must be one and the same entity. Thus, two numerically distinct entities cannot be exactly similar. The thesis of the indiscernibility of identicals is that if x and y are identical, then they have all and only the same properties in common. Thus, if x and y differ with respect to some property, then x and y cannot be one and the same.

Leibniz's law has played an important role in various discussions of, for instance, PHYSICALISM and DUALISM, since it imposes a requirement on the distinction between mental and physical entities that there be something true of one that is not true of the other. Much of the discussion concerning Leibniz's law in the context of arguments for dualism concerns whether arguments with dualistic conclusions are valid and contain legitimate applications of Leibniz's law or instead involve commission of the INTENSIONAL FALLACY. *See also* INTENSIONALITY; INTENSION (WITH AN "S").

linguistic determinism, also known as the SAPIR–WHORF HYPOTHESIS, the thesis that what kinds of THOUGHT, BELIEF, and PERCEPTION one is capable of having are dependent on features of the language one speaks. One version of linguistic determinism would hold that speakers who differ in how many basic color words their language has would differ with respect to the kinds of perceptual color discriminations they can make. Most versions of the LANGUAGE OF THOUGHT hypothesis, especially those that posit a MENTALESE that one must possess prior to learning any spoken language, are logically distinct from the thesis of linguistic determinism. That is, one can subscribe to the existence of an innate Mentalese without thereby being committed to linguistic determinism. This is due to the fact that linguistic determinism is a thesis concerning noninnate, acquired languages.

logical positivism, sometimes just "positivism," a version of EMPIRICISM that became an especially prominent philosophical movement in the early twentieth century. One of the key theses of positivism was VERIFICATIONISM, especially as construed as a thesis about meaning. Positivists also were attracted to certain versions of reductionism (*see* REDUCTION), such as PHENOMENALISM (the reduction of so-called physical objects to SENSE DATA) and BEHAVIORISM (the reduction of mental states to behaviors or behavioral dispositions). Influential critiques of positivism were due to Wilfrid SELLARS and W.V.O. QUINE. Sellars attacked versions of the SENSE-DATUM THEORY and what he called "The Myth of the Given" (*see* GIVEN; GIVEN, MYTH OF THE). Quine attacked the analytic/synthetic distinction and phenomenalistic reductionism.

mark of the mental, an alleged property had by all and only mental phenomena. Franz BRENTANO famously offered INTENTIONALITY as the mark of the mental (*see also* BRENTANO'S THESIS). A relatively standard view opposed to Brentano's is that some mental states have QUALIA but no intentional CONTENT. Brentano's thesis that intentionality was the mark of the mental played a key role in his argument that the mental was irreducible to the physical (*see* REDUCTIONISM). The philosopher Richard Rorty argued that the mark of the mental is INCORRIGIBILITY (*see also* FIRST-PERSON AUTHORITY; PRIVILEGED ACCESS). Rorty's thesis that incorrigibility is the mark of the mental played a key role in his argument for ELIMINATIVE MATERIALISM, on the grounds that nothing is known incorrigibly.

materialism, see PHYSICALISM.

memory, a mental state of a subject due to, and sharing at least some CONTENT with, past episodes of the EXPERIENCE of that subject (where experience is understood as involving episodes of PERCEPTION and INTROSPECTION). Alternately, the capacity by which such mental states are enabled. The requirement that a subject's memories be due to some prior states of experience serves to distinguish memories from other kinds of BELIEF that happen to be about past events in the subject's life. For example, I have no memory of weighing nine pounds at birth, though I do have beliefs about my birth weight based on the testimony of my parents. These beliefs do not count as memories of my birth weight because of the lack of an appropriate causal continuity between my current belief and an experience of mine at the time of my birth. I likely had no experience of how much I weighed, and of the various experiences I did have at birth, no memory trace of my own survives.

mental causation, denied by EPIPHENOMENALISM, the having of effects, by mental phenomena, on any other phenomena, especially physical phenomena. An example would be the production of a bodily motion (a physical event) as a result of an episode of willing (*see* WILL, THE). (*See also* ACTION.) Another would be the causing of one mental state by another in a chain of REASONING. More broadly, mental causation concerns the causes of mental phenomena in addition to their effects. On this broader construal, an example would be the production of a PERCEPTION of an avalanche as a causal consequence of an avalanche. That mental phenomena enter into various causal interactions with one another and with nonmental phenomena is a core idea of many varieties of FUNCTIONALISM. For example, one sort of functionalistic thesis holds that what it is to be a BELIEF, and in particular a belief that *tigers have stripes*, is to be a state of a subject that has various causal relations to other states of the subject, including other states of belief as well as states of sensory reactions to striped tigers and states of intention toward certain kinds of behaviors concerning striped tigers. *See also* EXPLANATORY EXCLUSION; INTERACTIONISM.

mental representation, any mental entity having INTENTIONALITY or CONTENT; the VEHICLE that has the content. Alternately, a process—namely, the directing of the mind toward its contents. The two main issues of mental representation discussed by philosophers of mind concern (1) the means by which representations have their contents (*see* CONTENT, THEORIES OF) and (2) the format of mental representations (*see* COGNITIVE ARCHITECTURE). Regarding (2), the main competing positions debated are (a) that mental representations have a pictorial or an imagistic format (*see* IMAGERY), (b) that mental representations have a linguistic format (*see* LANGUAGE OF THOUGHT; SYMBOLICISM), and (c) that mental representations have a holographic or distributed format (*see* CONNECTIONISM).

Mentalese, the LANGUAGE OF THOUGHT conceived of as a language distinct from any of the languages that a thinker is able to speak or write. Mentalese is thus distinct from for example, English, French, etc. Some philosophers have held that while there is such a thing as a language of thought, it is simply an internalized version of the one or more languages that a thinker is able to speak. Such philosophers thus deny the existence of Mentalese while affirming the existence of a language of thought. One line of reasoning in favor of Mentalese is that if a language of thought is posited to explain, among other things, how a thinker learns their first spoken language, then the language of thought must be some distinct language from the one that is learned.

methodological solipsism, where INTERNALISM or INDIVIDUALISM is a thesis about what mental states *are* (namely, states whose natures are determined solely by what is in the brain or body of the subject of the mental states), methodological solipsism is a recommendation about how best to *study* and *explain* the intelligent behaviors of subjects—namely, by focusing solely on the causes of behavior having to do with what is in the brain or body of the subject.

mind/body problem, the problem of establishing whether there are such things as minds, such properties as mental properties, and, if so, specifying the nature of any relations that mental things and properties bear to physical bodies and physical properties. Key philosophical positions regarding the mind-body problem are DUALISM, PHYSICALISM and IDEALISM. See also "The Mind/ Body Problem" in the previous chapter, "Introduction: What Is Philosophy of Mind?"

missing shade of blue, a THOUGHT EXPERIMENT due to David HUME that potentially poses a problem for the brand of EMPIRICISM that Hume defended. The thought experiment involves a person who has seen many shades of blue except for one, the "missing shade of blue." According to one interpretation of empiricism, such a person could not grasp in THOUGHT such a missing shade of blue, since the *idea* of such a shade is a copy of the sensory IMPRESSION of the shade and, lacking a sensory experience of the shade would seem to prevent people from forming adequate CONCEPTS of the shade. Alternately, one might say that lacking experience of the missing shade of blue would, on this interpretation of empiricism, bar such a person from knowing WHAT IT IS LIKE to experience the missing shade of blue. However, Hume, as well as others following him, thought that it was implausible that one could not form an idea of the missing shade of blue without having experienced it. For a related puzzle for empiricism, *see* MOLYNEUX QUESTION.

modal argument, an argument against PHYSICALISM in which key roles are played by the modal concepts of *necessity* and POSSIBILITY or *contingency*. The basic gist of the argument involves arguing from premises concerning the necessity of identities (if x = y, then necessarily x = y) and the contingency of any relation between mental and physical properties. Since, allegedly, for any physical property, it is possible for it to be instantiated without any mental property to thereby be instantiated, no physical property is identical to any physical property. According to a version of the modal argument formulated by Saul KRIPKE, although all identities, if true, are necessarily true, some identities, such as the identities found in natural science (such as "Water is identical to H_2O") *seem* contingent. According to Kripke, the APPEARANCE of contingency for such identities can be explained away in the following manner: What is contingently related to H_2O is the watery appearance to us of H_2O. While H_2O is necessarily water, H_2O is not necessarily watery-appearing to us. So, any apparently contingent identity—that is, any apparently possible nonidentity—is not really a nonidentity if the appearance of contingency can be explained away in terms of a contingent relation between the appearance and the reality of a phenomenon. Contrapositively, if some *apparent* possible nonidentity cannot be explained away in such a manner, then it is a *real* nonidentity. Kripke offers that the apparent contingent relation between PAIN and neurophysiological events ("c-fibers firing") does not admit of any such explaining away. This is supposed to follow because, according to Kripke, anything that *appears* to the mind as a pain *just is* a pain: There is no distinction between the appearance of pain and the reality of pain. In versions of the modal argument due to David CHALMERS, the contingency of mental-physical relations is supposed to follow from the CONCEIVABILITY of hypothetical scenarios, such as the INVERTED SPECTRUM and the ZOMBIE. Like the KNOWLEDGE ARGUMENT and the EXPLANATORY GAP argument, the modal argument is an *epistemic-gap* argument against physicalism. All three arguments infer from a gap between the physical and the phenomenal that arises concerning what we can know, explain, or conceive (an epistemic gap), to a gap in ONTOLOGY between physical properties and phenomenal properties.

modularity, the hypothesis that at least some mental capacities are functionally localizable in distinct modules. According to Jerry FODOR, a particularly high-profile proponent of the modularity hypothesis, modules may be characterized in contrast to nonmodular systems as being, among other things, relatively (1) fast, (2) domain specific, and (3) "informationally encapsulated." Thus, to illustrate, peripheral perceptual systems and not central systems of THOUGHT and REASONING (1) deliver their outputs to other systems without drawing lengthy inferences (*see* INFERENCE), (2) are responsive to a relatively limited range of inputs, and (3) receive inputs from no other part of the mind (from neither another module nor the nonmodular central system).

Molyneux question, a question posed to John LOCKE by William Molyneux (1656–1698), a lawyer and member of the Irish Parliament, of whether a man blind from birth, knowing of shapes such as cubes and spheres only via his sense of touch, would, upon having his sight restored, recognize cubes and spheres as such by sight without having to go through a period of learning to associate his visual ideas of shape with his tactile ideas of shape. Conceptually, the Molyneux question is a close relative of a question one may raise concerning the central THOUGHT EXPERIMENT of the KNOWLEDGE ARGUMENT: Would someone who had never experienced red before nonetheless know WHAT IT'S LIKE? *See also* EMPIRICISM; MISSING SHADE OF BLUE.

monad, in the ONTOLOGY of Lebniz, the only substances (*see* SUBSTANCE) that existed were "monads"—nonmaterial entities lacking spatial parts, entering into no causal interactions with one another, and having no properties other than their various perceptions (*see* PERCEPTION) and appetites. Leibniz thus embraced an early version of PHENOMENALISM and explained away all apparent causation (including MENTAL CAUSATION) as instead due to PRE-ESTABLISHED HARMONY.

monism, any of a variety of views that have as their common core the thesis that there fundamentally exists only one sort of thing. Examples include physicalist monism (*see* PHYSICALISM), idealist monism (*see* IDEALISM), and neutral monism (*see* MONISM, NEUTRAL). Two versions of physicalist monism are the view that everything is physical and mental things do not exist (*see* ELIMINATIVE MATERIALISM) and the view that mental things do exist and are really a kind of physical thing (*see* PHYSICALISM, REDUCTIVE). Versions of idealist monism include the view that everything is mental and thus physical things either do not exist or are really a kind of mental thing (*see* IDEALISM; *see also* PHENOMENALISM). Neutral monism is the view that the one sort of fundamentally existing thing is neither mental nor physical. Monism is opposed to DUALISM.

monism, neutral, a variety of MONISM opposed to both physicalist monism (*see* PHYSICALISM) and idealist monism (*see* IDEALISM) in holding that while there is only one fundamentally existing sort of thing, it is neither physical nor mental. Adherents of neutral monism include Bertrand Russell, who held both mental and physical entities to be logical constructs out of more fundamental neutral entities.

Moore's paradox, due to G. E. Moore, a puzzling type of scenario concerning utterances expressing a conjunction of a description of a STATE OF AFFAIRS being the case and an announcement that the state of affairs is not *believed* to be the case by the speaker. One such example would be someone saying "It is raining and I do not believe it is raining." Since the first conjunct, "It is raining," is asserted sincerely only by speakers who believe that it is raining, there's an apparent tension that arises between such a belief and the belief seemingly expressed by the second conjunct, "I do not believe it is raining." *See also* FIRST PERSON.

multiple-drafts theory of consciousness, due to Daniel DENNETT, a theory of CONSCIOUSNESS consistent with PHYSICALISM wherein a conscious state (*see* CONSCIOUSNESS, STATE) is spread out in both space and time in the brain across multiple instances of what Dennett calls "content fixations" (*see* MENTAL REPRESENTATION), each of which—the "multiple drafts"—compete for domination in the cognitive system or what Dennett calls "fame in the brain." Crucial to Dennett's account of consciousness is a denial of the existence of what he calls "the Cartesian theater"—a single place in the brain where at some specific time which is the onset of consciousness, "it all comes together." The Cartesian theater is where the various previously unconscious brain events march onto the stage of consciousness before the audience of a HOMUNCULUS who watches the passing show. Dennett regards such a positing of a homunculus as nonexplanatory: How is the homunculus conscious of the show in the Cartesian theater?

Many of the considerations that Dennett provides in support of the multiple-drafts theory hinge on features concerning the application of the CONTENT/VEHICLE DISTINCTION to conscious representations of time. Such representations may themselves (the *vehicles*) occur at times other than the times that they are representations of (the *contents*). The importance of the content/vehicle distinction for time representation can be drawn out in contemplation of an argument Dennett gives concerning the illusory motion and illusory color-change in an effect known as *the color-phi phenomenon*. In the color-phi phenomenon, the subject is presented with a brief flash of a green circle, followed by a brief flash of a red circle. The two flashes occur in slightly different locations. Subjects report the appearance of motion: a green circle, that moves and becomes red at the point roughly between where the green circle was flashed and where the red circle was flashed. Especially interesting is that subjects report that the green circle turns red before arriving at the spot where the red circle is flashed. The subjects cannot have known ahead of time that a red circle was going to flash, so how is it that they are able to have a conscious experience of something turning to red prior to the red circle's flashing? One candidate explanation is that the subject unconsciously perceives the red circle's flash and the subject's brain uses that INFORMATION to generate an illusory conscious experience of a green circle changing to red. Another candidate explanation is that the subject consciously perceived only the nonmoving green and red circle flashes and has a false memory of there having been a moving and color-shifting circle. Dennett argues that there is absolutely no basis for preferring one of these candidate explanations over the other. According to Dennett, there is no fact of the matter about consciousness aside from how things seem to the subject (*see* APPEARANCE), and how things seem to the subject is determined by the BELIEF that is arrived at via the process, smeared out in space and time in the brain, of competitions for fame in the brain via multiple content fixations. Some of Dennett's critics have accused his argument here of relying on an untenable VERIFICATIONISM.

multiple realizability, closely associated with FUNCTIONALISM, the idea that mental phenomena may arise in several different substrates and perhaps even nonphysical substrates. A common presumption among physicalists (*see* PHYSICALISM) is that a human has mental states, such as a BELIEF or a PAIN, in virtue of certain physical things happening inside of the body, specifically, inside of the nervous system. If it is possible for a belief or a pain to be realized in a very different physical system, such as a ROBOT, which has a computer "brain" made out of silicon and gallium arsenide (instead of the lipids and proteins that constitute human brains), then mental states may have multiple physical realizations. Further, if it is possible for a belief or a pain to be realized not only in physical substrates such as the brains of humans, but also in the non-physical "ectoplasm" of which ghosts are composed, then mental states may have nonphysical realizations as well.

Examples of possible physical multiple realizations that philosophers of mind have discussed besides the nonorganism cases of robots include nonhuman organism cases such as octopi, which may feel pain despite having quite different nervous systems from humans, and nonterrestrial cases of beings from other planets, beings that may have very different biochemistries from terrestrial creatures.

Multiple realizability is frequently mobilized in arguments for functionalism and against (type-) IDENTITY THEORY. One way of illustrating the connection between multiple realizability and functionalism is via contemplation of the following THOUGHT EXPERIMENT: Suppose that, via some futuristic procedure, a person were to have their various organs replaced with prostheses made of metal and plastic that nonetheless were able to perform the same functions as their biological analogues (*see* FUNCTION, TELEOLOGICAL). Sensory organs such as eyes could be replaced with digital cameras, and ears could be replaced with sensitive microphones. The replacement of the entire central nervous system could be accomplished by a gradual procedure whereby, one-by-one, each neuron in the nervous system is replaced by a silicon microchip that performs the exact same function as the biological unit it replaces. Suppose that, at the end of such a procedure, the now fully mechanized human still has various mental states despite having them in virtue of a very different physical realization. The question arises as to what it is that remained the same in virtue of which the mental states remained. And here a natural answer is that although certain physical parts were replaced, the crucial element that remained the same is that the replacements still performed the same *function*.

Multiple realizability has also figured in arguments for property dualism (*see* DUALISM, PROPERTY). If two systems that count as multiple realizations of the same mental property share *none* of their physical properties, then the mental property in question cannot be identical to any physical property.

myth of the given, *see* GIVEN, MYTH OF THE.

nativism, any of a class of views holding some mental item or capacity to be innate. *See* INNATENESS.

natural kind, a grouping of entities into a collection that is not gerrymandered but instead "carves nature at the joints." A plausible example of a natural kind is the chemical kind *acid*. In contrast, the set of all of the objects in the universe that were within sixty yards of my left ankle on Friday, November 14, 2008 is not a plausible example of a natural kind. (See the discussion of the concept *game* in the entry on FAMILY RESEMBLANCE.) It is a matter of controversy whether there really are any good ways of distinguishing natural kinds from nonnatural kinds. While some philosophers are skeptical of the distinction between natural and nonnatural kinds, others see as a clear example of a natural kind the collection of all hydrogen atoms and as a clear example of a nonnatural kind the collection of all objects that have ever been within three feet of a drawing of an umbrella. The philosopher Richard Boyd has offered that natural kinds are homeostatic property clusters (sets of properties that serve to promote their continued coinstantiation (*see* PROPERTY; INSTANTIATION). Some philosophers of mind have been concerned with the question of whether folk-psychological kinds are sufficiently natural to sustain a SCIENTIFIC REALISM about mental kinds or whether instead an ELIMINATIVE MATERIALISM is a superior position.

naturalism, the view that at least some aspects of philosophy should be modeled after the natural sciences. Construed as a methodological recommendation, naturalism is the view that philosophers should regard as warranted only beliefs that may be justified utilizing the means of the natural sciences. Thus will naturalists typically emphasize empirical means of justification, such as justification by reference to observation and experimentation, and typically be suspicious of nonempirical means of justification, such as certain construals of INTUITION. Construed as an ontological recommendation, naturalism is the view that philosophers should not believe in the existence of any entity not countenanced by the natural sciences.

The ontological construal of naturalism is closely associated with PHYSICALISM, at least insofar as many avowed naturalists are also avowed physicalists. However, some controversy surrounds the proposal that a physicalistic monism is the most natural choice for a naturalist. David CHALMERS promotes a naturalistic form of DUALISM. And in an earlier era, many adherents of LOGICAL POSITIVISM could be described as naturalists who subscribed to either a phenomenalistic form of IDEALISM (*see* PHENOMENALISM) or a neutral monism (*see* MONISM, NEUTRAL).

One of the most influential advocates of naturalism was W.V.O. QUINE, who argued persuasively for the continuity of philosophy and the natural sciences with respect to both method and subject matter.

neural network, a biological system or subsystem comprising all or part of a creature's nervous system and constituted by a collection of interconnected cells, including neurons (cells directly involved in relaying electrochemical signals throughout the nervous system) and glial cells ("support cells" that provide nutrients and oxygen to neurons). A creature's nervous system may be alternately thought of as a single neural network or as multiple connected networks.

Alternately, a neural network is a mathematical abstraction or computer simulation loosely based on biological systems wherein multiple interconnected units, so-called neurons, undergo state-transitions as a result of influences propagated along the various connections between units. Different connections may be differently "weighted" and thus may different degrees of influence be propagated along the connections. Various techniques exist for modeling learning in such networks. *See also* CONNECTIONISM.

Many adherents of the TYPE-IDENTITY THESIS subscribe to the view that mental state types may be identified with types of activity in a human's neural network. One common illustration used by philosophers of such a type-identity is the identification of PAIN with *c-fibers firing*, although this is probably an inaccurate oversimplification of the relevant neuroscience. With the advent of a more widespread interest in NEUROPHILOSOPHY since the mid-1980s many philosophers of mind have pursued detailed investigations of the relevance of various aspects of neural networks to an understanding of the mind.

neurophilosophy, due to Patricia CHURCHLAND, a version of NATURALISM wherein the embrace of a continuity between philosophy and the natural sciences is primarily concerned with the continuity of philosophy and the *neurosciences*. Some philosophers have distinguished neurophilosophy from the *philosophy of neuroscience*, defining the former as the application of neuroscience to philosophy (resulting in, for example, a kind of philosophy of mind) and the latter as the philosophical investigation of neuroscience (resulting in a kind of philosophy of science). Others, including Patricia Churchland, do not endorse this restricted use of the term "neurophilosophy." (*See also* Paul CHURCHLAND.)

Neurophilosophers tend to be attracted to either reductive physicalism (*see* PHYSICALISM, REDUCTIVE) or ELIMINATIVE MATERIALISM with respect to the mind-body problem and CONNECTIONISM with respect to COGNITIVE ARCHITECTURE. It should be noted, however, that neurophilosophy does not consist simply in adhering to one or more of the above-named positions, for many philosophers hold positions such as reductive physicalism without thereby being neurophiloso-phers. One way of appreciating what's distinctive about neurophilosophy is not so much the conclusions reached but the *means* by which they are reached—that is, the premises from which such conclusions are argued. Distinctive, then, of neurophilosophy is a reliance on findings in neuroscience for the drawing of conclusions of pertinence to various philosophical investi-gations (be they in philosophy of mind, philosophy of science, or some other philosophical branch).

nonconceptual content, CONTENT, the possession of which may be had without possessing the CONCEPTS that would be required in order either to say what the content is, or express in a language a THOUGHT concerning such a content. One way of appreciating the philosophical technical notion of non-conceptual content is in terms of states of creatures that satisfy criteria for having INTENTIONALITY or having a MENTAL REPRESENTATION without the intentional or representational STATE in question satisfying criteria on concepts such as the criterion known as the GENERALITY CONSTRAINT. According to some philosophers, an animal incapable of using language but capable of perceptually discrimi-nating red from nonred objects has states with nonconceptual content concerning redness but lacks any concept of, or conceptualized thought about, redness. Another consideration that some philosophers take to favor the postulation of nonconceptual content is the claim that even language-using humans have experiences of, for example, shades of color that may be discriminated in EXPERIENCE in a way that is more fine-grained than any distinctions they can make at the level of conceptual thought.

Some philosophers discussing nonconceptual content have pointed out that at least some of the concerns discussed under the heading "nonconceptual content" are not so much about a distinctive kind of content but instead about a distinctive kind of mental state. On certain conceptions of content, such as those advocated by certain externalists (*see* EXTERNALISM), whatever differences there might be between perception and conceptual thought is not what their contents are, since contents are just certain things in the external world (or the bearing of certain relations to certain things in the external world) and the external objects that can be related to in perception can also be related to in thought. Thus, if there are important differences between perception and thought having to do with, for example, differences in fineness of grain, these may instead be differences of state instead of content (*see* CONTENT/VEHICLE DISTINCTION).

normative, pertaining to the way things *ought* to be, which may be distinguished from the *descriptive,* which pertains to the way things *are.* That the normative is distinct from the descriptive is a point that many trace back to HUME and is often expressed by the slogan "You cannot derive an 'ought' from an 'is'." Much of the traditional discussion of the Humean point concerned its application to various moral discussions. For example, the Humean sort of point may be raised against moral theories that would try to define immorality as the causing of PAIN: to say that someone is in pain is to describe an empirically knowable state of affairs. But it is not clear that from that description one can derive any recommendation about what one *ought* to do. Why does it follow from one's being in pain that someone *ought* to act to make the pain stop? Why does it follow from the POSSIBILITY of future pain that one *ought* to act now for its prevention? Of course, if a person has a DESIRE to avoid pain, then there's a sense of "ought" wherein *that person* ought to avoid pain: They have a REASON to avoid pain. But this point seems not to capture the moral use of "ought" wherein, according to many moral philosophers, what *ought* to be the case is not directly determined by what anyone happens to desire to be the case.

While the above remarks mostly concern philosophical issues in ethics and only concern philosophy of mind indirectly (via notions central to PRACTICAL REASONING such as *desire*), some philosophers have sought to employ the notion of normativity in a much more direct way to issues in the philosophy of mind. Some philosophers, such as Donald DAVIDSON, Daniel DENNETT, and Wilfrid SELLARS hold that ascriptions of INTENTIONALITY and RATIONALITY are not merely descriptive and are ineliminably normative. To say, for example, that so-and-so has a THOUGHT with such-and-such CONTENT is not merely to describe some state of affairs, but to say that as a member of some community, they *ought* to behave in such-and-such way (and also have such-and-such other thoughts [*see* HOLISM]). *See also* ANOMALOUS MONISM; INTENTIONAL STANCE, THE.

objectivity, (1) of that which exists, that it exists independently of anyone's PERCEPTION of it or THOUGHT or BELIEF about it. (2) Of that which exists, KNOWLEDGE about it being acquirable via multiple kinds of EXPERIENCE. (3) Of mental states, especially judgments or beliefs, that they are arrived at impartially and do not simply reflect the bias of the judge or believer and, additionally, have their TRUTH value (true or false) in virtue of factors that have objectivity in sense (1) of the term "objectivity." All three senses of "objectivity" may be contrasted against correlative senses of SUBJECTIVITY.

Despite sense (3)'s being explicitly about a feature of mental states, senses (1) and (2) have played more central roles in the philosophy of mind. Sense (1) of "objectivity" has played a central role in discussions of REALISM and TRUTH. The classical debate between early versions of MATERIALISM and IDEALISM concerned whether so-called material objects existed independently of anyone's perceiving them or conceiving of them. Related are discussions of the contrast between PRIMARY QUALITIES and SECONDARY QUALITIES, with the former being more objective than the latter.

Sense (2) of "objectivity" and a contrasting sense of "subjectivity" have been central in discussions of phenomenal consciousness (*see* CONSCIOUSNESS, PHENO-MENAL). Some philosophers have urged that WHAT IT IS LIKE to see red or to be a bat is subjective in the sense of being knowable only from the point of view of one who has seen red or been a bat. In contrast, one need not have any particular kind of experience to know about the *brain states* of a bat or of a person seeing red. It is claimed, for instance, that while a person blind from birth may not know what it is like to see red, everything physical about the brain states of a red-seeing person is knowable by the blind person. (*See also* FIRST-PERSON; FIRST-PERSON AUTHORITY.)

occasionalism, due to Nicolas Malebranche (1638–1715), a version of substance dualism (*see* DUALISM, SUBSTANCE) whereby, although there is no causal interaction between mental substances and physical substances, any seeming psycho-physical interaction is actually due to God's continual intervention: God is the only true cause of any event. *See also* MENTAL CAUSATION; EPIPHENOMENALISM.

ontology, the branch of philosophy concerning the nature of existence and the most general categories of items that exist (e.g., objects, properties, events). Alternately, the ontology of a theory is the collection of entities required to exist in order for the theory to be true. *See also* STATE; PROPERTY; EVENT; STATE OF AFFAIRS.

opacity, referential, the failure of co-referring terms to be inter-substitutable without affecting the TRUTH value of the sentences they appear in. So, for example, in the sentence "John wrote 'Mark Twain is cool' on the board," the term "Samuel Clemens," despite having the same referent as "Mark Twain" will, if substituted for "Samuel Clemens," result in a sentence with a differing truth value. *See also* TRANSPARENCY, REFERENTIAL.

other minds, problem of, the problem of articulating the justification, if any, for the commonsense conviction that there exist minds other than one's own. The problem is especially vexing if one assumes that one may have empirical knowledge only of physical bodies and one knows of one's own mind directly via INTROSPECTION. (*See* FIRST-PERSON AUTHORITY.) It is unsatisfactory to attempt to ground knowledge of other minds by building on these assumptions and adding an argument by analogy wherein one notes correlations between one's own mental states and one's own behavior and conjectures that analogous behaviors in others involve analogous mental states. Such an inference constitutes a very hasty generalization, depending as it does on an inductive base of only a single sample. Some versions of FUNCTIONALISM and BEHAVIORISM attempt to account for knowledge of other minds as being on par with knowledge of one's own mind by, for example, treating knowledge of all minds as involving theoretical posits for the EXPLANATION of observable behaviors (*see* FOLK PSYCHOLOGY). Along such lines, Wilfrid SELLARS argued that one's knowledge of one's own mind is no less theoretical than one's knowledge of other minds. *See also* THEORY OF MIND.

pain, a bodily SENSATION, often, but not always, associated with tissue damage or tissue disturbance and often, but not always, unpleasant. That pains are not always associated with tissue damage or disturbance is evidenced by anesthetic conditions wherein tissue may be damaged or disturbed without giving rise to pain as well as so-called phantom pains (associated, in some instances, with the phantom-limb phenomenon that afflicts some amputees) wherein one may feel pain "in" a bodily region wherein there is no disturbance to or damage of any tissue in that region. That pains aren't always unpleasant is evidenced by certain anesthetic conditions wherein one may be aware of pain but not find it bothersome. As with other sensations, controversy surrounds the issue of whether pains have INTENTIONALITY or, instead, count as mental solely in virtue of nonintentional QUALIA. According to one sort of view (see, for example, FIRST-ORDER REPRESENTATIONALISM) a pain is a MENTAL REPRESENTATION of damage or disturbance of tissue in one's own body.

panpsychism, the view that mind is everywhere. While IDEALISM, the view that everything is mental, is a form of panpsychism, nonidealistic forms of panpsychism are possible as well, since it is possible to agree with the panpsychist that every location contains something mental while affirming, in opposition against the idealist, that some locations contain something nonmental as well.

perception, the apprehension, by the mind, of things other than itself. Thus characterized, perception is distinguished from INTROSPECTION, which is the mind's apprehension of itself. Sensory perception of things and events external to the perceiver's body is exteroception, and sensory perception of internal bodily things and events is interoception. Most, if not all, perception is sensory perception, there being no noncontroversial evidence for extrasensory perception.

There are various illuminating contrasts between perception and various kinds of other mental states: perception vs. SENSATION, perception vs. THOUGHT, and perception vs. IMAGERY. Regarding the contrast with sensation, there is a tradition in the philosophy of mind of regarding sensation as raw, uninterpreted (unconceptualized) input and perception the result of the application of one or more CONCEPTS to the sensational inputs. (Note, however, that controversy surrounds the claim that all perception is conceptual. See NONCONCEPTUAL CONTENT; SEEING, NONEPISTEMIC.) The distinction between sensation and perception aids in understanding the distinction between perception and thought. While both perception and thought may be viewed as varieties of PROPOSITIONAL ATTITUDE, it is the association with sensations that distinguishes perceptions from thoughts. It remains, then, to distinguish perception from imagery. One account of the contrast is that imagery is more directly under the control of the will (*see* WILL, THE) than is perception.

One line of inquiry concerning perception that philosophers have been interested in has to do with what the objects of perception are (the things that are perceived) and what the relation is between the perceiver and the perceptual object. *See* DIRECT REALISM; REPRESENTATIVE REALISM; IDEALISM.

perceptual relativity, the relativity of what is perceived or how it is perceived to the CONCEPTS, language, or prior PERCEPTION of the perceiver. Illustrations of relativity to a *prior perception* come from instances of perceptual adaptation, such as when tepid water feels hot when felt with a hand previously in cool water and feels cold when felt with a hand previously in hot water. For discussions of relativity to *language*, see the entries on LINGUISTIC DETERMINISM and the SAPIR–WHORF HYPOTHESIS. Regarding relativity to *concepts*, many philosophers hold that the case for such relativity is stronger when applied to *fact perception* than when applied to *object perception*. Such philosophers hold it to be plausible that it is a requirement on seeing *that* a dog is in the yard (fact perception) that one grasps the concept of dogs. Meanwhile, they hold it to be implausible that it is a requirement on seeing *a dog* (object perception) that one grasps the concept of dogs. Such philosophers may hold that the first kind of seeing is to be distinguished from the second in that the first (seeing *that* a dog is in the yard) is *epistemic* seeing (*see* SEEING, EPISTEMIC) and the second (seeing *a dog* without grasping the concept of dogs) is *nonepistemic* seeing (*see* SEEING, NONEPISTEMIC).

personal identity, the numerical identity of a person, especially as considered over time; a person's being, at one time, one and the same person as a person at another time. I was once only ten pounds, and it may seem puzzling, especially with LEIBNIZ'S LAW in mind, how it is that an entity that is *not* ten pounds (an entity such as I am) can be one and the same entity as an entity that *is* ten pounds (an entity such as I was as a baby). Despite my having changed with respect to my weight, and in other ways besides, how is it that I remain one and the same person? One classical theory of personal identity is due to John LOCKE, who held that what determines the continuity of a person's identity over time is not due to the identity over time of a single SUBSTANCE (either material or immaterial), but of a continuity between the various memories of a person over time (*see* MEMORY).

phase space, alternately, a STATE space, an abstract space representing, of some system, the various dimensions along which possible changes may occur to that system. So, for example, a system describable in terms of changes in temperature, pressure, and volume may be characterized by a three-dimensional phase space or state space wherein each point in that space represents a particular combination of temperature, pressure, and volume. The notion of a phase space has figured in both CONNECTIONISM and DYNAMIC SYSTEMS THEORY.

phenomenal concepts, minimally, CONCEPTS utilized in thinking about the phenomenal character of conscious states (*see* QUALIA). Typically, "phenomenal concepts" is reserved for an allegedly special kind of concept of phenomenal character, a kind of concept posited to explain, for example, why it is that a person blind from birth cannot know WHAT IT IS LIKE to see red (*see* KNOWLEDGE ARGUMENT): such a person may be able to conceive of what it's like to see red in various ways (e.g., by conceiving of it as "that thing that Mandik is talking about when he talks about what it is like to see red"), but not in the *special* way required for knowing what it's like to see red. Some defenders of PHYSICAL-ISM have been attracted to the suggestion that by positing the existence of phenomenal concepts, physicalists can block the knowledge argument against physicalism. One way of conveying the strategy is by saying that what a person seeing red for the first time gains is not access to a new kind of fact, but a new way of conceptualizing an old fact.

phenomenalism, a kind of IDEALISM wherein so-called physical objects are asserted to be nothing more than certain patterns of sensory EXPERIENCE. Alternately, the view that statements about so-called material objects could be translated into statements about what sequences of sensations (*see* SENSATION) would follow from some initial sensation. *See also* EMPIRICISM; LOGICAL POSITIVISM.

phenomenology, the philosophical study of APPEARANCE, CONSCIOUSNESS, or WHAT IT IS LIKE as regarded from the FIRST-PERSON point of view. Alternately, what it is like to be some particular or kind of subject, as regarded from the first-person point of view. An example of this second usage would be: "For all I know, bat phenomenology is very different from human phenomenology and my own brother may have color phenomenology completely inverted relative to my own." *See also* FIRST-PERSON AUTHORITY.

phi phenomenon, a perceptual illusion involving a PERCEPTION of illusory motion induced by the presentation of a succession of flashed yet nonmoving stimuli, as in the lights on a marquee. For example, if a red spot is flashed briefly then followed by a red spot of similar size but different location being flashed, subjects will report seeing a single spot moving from the location of the first spot to the location of the second spot. An especially interesting version of the phi phenomenon, known as "color phi," was suggested by the philosopher Nelson Goodman and involves the two flashed stimuli differing in color. Subjects report, for instance, a green dot changing its color to red midway through its trajectory. Part of what's puzzling about color phi can be conveyed by pointing out that the brain or mind of the perceiver cannot know what color to change the initially green dot to until *after* the red dot appears. However, from the FIRST-PERSON point of view, what's perceived is first a green dot, then a green dot changing to a red dot, then the red dot arriving at its final position. Discussion of color phi plays a prominent role in the development of the MULTIPLE DRAFTS THEORY OF CONSCIOUSNESS of Daniel DENNETT.

physicalism, in its most inclusive sense, the view that everything is determined by the physical, though it may be left open whether everything *is* physical. This inclusive conception of physicalism allows for nonreductive physicalism (*see* PHYSICALISM, NONREDUCTIVE). On a more restrictive conception of physicalism, only ELIMINATIVE MATERIALISM and reductive physicalism (*see* PHYSICALISM, REDUCTIVE) count as versions of physicalism.

Probably not enough is said in most discussions of physicalism about what it means to *be physical*. One sort of approach to this problem is to identify the physical with the basic entities and properties of contemporary physics. But such an approach is not without its problems. One problem is that many of what may be regarded as prototypical instances of physical objects, such as rocks, turn out not to be physical, since the subatomic particles of which rocks are constituted, but not the rocks themselves, count as basic entities in contemporary physics. Another problem is that it is likely that contemporary physics awaits further revision as further discoveries are made and many views currently held about what to count as basic entities, and properties will eventually be rejected as false. The defender of physicalism may be tempted to respond to such a worry that what should be regarded as physical is not what *is* accepted by *current* physics but what *will be* accepted by a *final, completed,* physics. But this leads to another problem. Such a view leaves open the possibility that prototypically nonphysical entities, such as QUALIA, will count among the basic, nonreducible features of existence (*see* DUALISM). According to many views, such a scenario would count as a vindication of dualism. However, if the final physicists agree that there exist nonreducible qualia, then, on at least one definition of "physical," it would seem that qualia would turn out to be physical.

physicalism, nonreductive, the view that while everything has physical properties and that all properties are determined by physical properties, there are some properties that are not identical to any physical properties or collections of physical properties. Thus is nonreductive physicalism consistent with property dualism (*see* DUALISM, PROPERTY). *See also* SUPERVENIENCE; ANOMALOUS MONISM; TOKEN-IDENTITY THESIS.

physicalism, reductive, the view that all properties are identical to physical properties or collections of physical properties. Reductive physicalists, unlike adherents of ELIMINATIVE MATERIALISM, typically affirm the existence of mental properties. *See also* TYPE-IDENTITY THEORY.

possibility, that which is not but might be, as well as that which *is* (since actualities are possibilities, in virtue of not being impossibilities). *See also* POSSIBLE WORLD. Discussion of possibility is pervasive throughout many areas of philosophy. Especially prominent in philosophy of mind have been discussions concerning the relations between possibility and CONCEIVABILITY. One oft-discussed line of thought against certain versions of PHYSICALISM might be summarized as follows: If QUALIA are identical to some neural properties, then it is impossible, for instance, to have those neural properties instantiated without any qualia being thereby instantiated (*see* ZOMBIE). By contraposition, if it is possible to have those neural properties without any qualia, then qualia cannot be identical to those neural properties. Is there any reason to believe in such a possibility? Some philosophers have defended the view that if a situation is *conceivable*, then it is possible. *See also* MODAL ARGUMENT.

possible world, a coherent set of ways the world can be. There exists at least one possible world, namely the actual world, and if there exist ways in which the world can be other than the way it actually is, then there exist other possible worlds besides the actual world. Multiple nonactual possible worlds are postulated by some philosophers to serve as truth-makers for statements such as "Jones didn't actually win the race, but he could have." Explicated in terms of possible worlds, our example statement is made true by the fact that in the actual world Jones lost the race and that there exists at least one nonactual world in which Jones (or Jones's trans-world counterpart) wins the race (or the race's trans-world counterpart).

poverty of the stimulus, an argument, due to Noam CHOMSKY, against BEHAVIORISM, especially as applied to the learning of a speaker's first language, which says that language acquisition cannot simply be due to the conditioning of responses to stimuli because the pattern of linguistic behaviors exhibited by early language learners far outstrips any stimuli that they were exposed to. For example, the young speakers may say certain things even though they were never previously rewarded for saying those things nor exposed to any-one else saying those things. In such a way are the stimuli involved in language acquisition "impoverished."

practical reasoning, figuring out what to *do* as opposed to what to *believe*; REASONING directed toward ACTION instead of BELIEF.

pre-established harmony, a view due to Leibniz wherein there is no causal interaction between the mental and the physical and any synchrony between mental and physical events is due to God's having created the mental and physical to act in concert. *See also* EPIPHENOMENALISM.

primary qualities, a kind of PROPERTY of material objects, distinguished by John LOCKE from SECONDARY QUALITIES and characterized by inhering in objects in themselves as opposed to depending on the PERCEPTION of the objects. Typical examples of primary qualities include those defined spatially, such as the size and shape of the objects.

private-language argument, due to Ludwig WITTGENSTEIN, an argument the conclusion of which is that it is impossible for there to be a language that can be understood by only a single individual. Another way to put the conclusion, then, is that if a language may be understood by *any* individual, then it must be possible as well for it to be understood by *many* individuals. Wittgenstein's discussion of the argument involves contemplation of an attempt to devise a language for keeping a diary of one's own private sensations. A key issue that arises is, in devising a sign, "S," to stand for some particular SENSATION, whether there can be any basis for knowing or saying that "S" does indeed stand for that sensation as opposed to something else or nothing at all. The keeper of the allegedly private journal will not be in a position to distinguish whether his grasp of a private ostensive definition of "S" is correct instead of merely *seeming* correct. And where there can be no graspable distinction between seeming correct and being correct, there is no place for a notion of correctness at all (*see also* NORMATIVE).

privileged access, *see* FIRST-PERSON AUTHORITY.

pro attitude, any of a class of mental states that constitute or contribute to a favorable disposition toward some end (toward some STATE OF AFFAIRS) or toward some object. Examples include DESIRE, INTENTION, hoping, and wishing. *See also* ACTION; WILL, THE.

problem of other minds, *see* OTHER MINDS, PROBLEM OF.

problem of the speckled hen, an objection, posed by Gilbert RYLE, against the SENSE-DATUM THEORY of PERCEPTION, namely that an implausible consequence of the theory is that when one perceives a speckled hen, one has an immediate awareness of a sense-datum that has a determinate number of speckles. While it is plausible that one can be aware of something as having many speckles, it is implausible that, if the precise number of speckles is 132, that one is aware of a thing as having precisely 132 speckles.

productivity, a capacity of thinkers to think an indefinite or potentially infinite number of thoughts. Along with SYSTEMATICITY, productivity is one of the features of thought alleged by Jerry FODOR to be common among thinkers and best explained by hypothesizing a LANGUAGE OF THOUGHT. The language-of-thought hypothesis accounts for productivity by postulating a finite store of combinable items akin to words in a spoken or written language that admit of an indefinite or potentially infinite number of combinations. Consider, for example, a representational system for representing numbers, such as the decimal system. The decimal system utilizes a finite store of basic symbols: the decimal point, the minus sign, and the ten numerals ("0" through "9,"). Additionally, the system incorporates rules for creating sequences of numerals (such as the rule that implies that "100.99" and "–42.3" but not "100.99.9" count as well formed). Such a system allows for the representation of a potentially infinite number of numbers. Similarly, a language with truth-functional logical operators and symbols for atomic sentences allows for the formulation of a potentially infinite number of complex representations: "P & ~Q," "~(P & ~Q)," "~~(P & ~Q)," "~~~(P & ~Q)," and so on. A thinker exhibits productivity, for example, by being able to think an indefinite number of thoughts such as *Mary kissed John, Mary did not kiss John, Mary did not not kiss John*, and so on.

property, a UNIVERSAL that may be instantiated (*see* INSTANTIATION) by multiple numerically distinct things. Thus, two red apples instantiate one and the same property: redness. Properties, such as the property of redness, are thought to be distinct from both the predicative expression "is red," which is a linguistic item, and the concept of redness (*see* CONCEPTS), which (according to some) is a mental item. Thus is the property of redness thought to be something "in the world" distinct from linguistic or mental representations of the things in the world. However, though distinct from representations, some properties at least may nonetheless depend on relations to representations. In connection with this latter sort of suggestion, see the entry on SECONDARY QUALITIES.

Alternate views of properties deny that they are universals and thus conceive of the redness of one apple as a numerically distinct redness (a TROPE) from the redness of a numerically distinct apple.

proposition, a nonlinguistic abstract entity expressed by distinct declarative sentences that express the same thing, as in the English "Snow is white" and the German "Schnee ist weiss." Propositions are further conceived of as the primary bearers of TRUTH values (truth and falsity) such that true declarative sentences are true in virtue of expressing true propositions and false declarative sentences are false in virtue of expressing false propositions.

The main significance of propositions for the philosophy of mind is that they are that to which PROPOSITIONAL ATTITUDES are attitudes toward.

Among philosophers who believe in the existence of such abstract entities as propositions, controversy exists concerning just what sort of abstract entities they are. One sort of proposal appeals to possible worlds (*see* POSSIBLE WORLD). For instance, perhaps the proposition expressed by "Snow is white" is merely the set of all possible worlds wherein there is snow and it is white. Another sort of proposal is that propositions are complex entities with structures mirroring the structures of the sentences expressing them. For example, the sentence "Bill Clinton is human" is composed of a name "Bill Clinton," which denotes an individual, and a predicative phrase, "is human," which picks out the property of being human. One sort of proposal for what proposition is expressed by "Bill Clinton is human" is that it is an ordered pair that has Bill Clinton as its first member and the property of being human as its second member. A different version of this sort of proposal would have the members be, instead of Bill Clinton and the property of being human, modes of presentation or senses (*see* SENSE) that mediate between thinkers and, respectively, Bill Clinton and the property of being human.

propositional attitude, a mental state such as a BELIEF or a DESIRE that involves a relation (the attitude) that a thinker bears toward a PROPOSITION. In desiring to drink beer and believing that there is beer in the refrigerator, George adopts an attitude of desire toward the proposition *George drinks beer* and adopts an attitude of belief toward the proposition *There is beer in the refrigerator*. Propositional attitudes are paradigmatic examples of mental states with INTENTIONALITY. According to the LANGUAGE OF THOUGHT hypothesis, having a propositional attitude involves bearing a relation to a complex entity that is a sentence in one's own language of thought. According to some versions of ELIMINATIVE MATERIALISM, propositional attitudes are useless fictions in a discredited FOLK PSYCHOLOGY that will be supplanted by a perfected neuroscience (*see also* NEUROPHILOSOPHY).

propositional knowledge, KNOWLEDGE *that* such-and-such is the case; knowledge of the TRUTH of some PROPOSITION. Many philosophers hold propositional knowledge to be a form of knowledge distinct from, for example, KNOWLEDGE BY ACQUAINTANCE and procedural knowledge, also known as KNOW-HOW.

prototype theory, a theory of concepts that denies that concepts can be analyzed into sets of necessary and sufficient conditions for the correct application of the concept (*see* CONCEPTUAL ANALYSIS) and instead affirms that concepts have their application criteria in virtue of a graded structure consisting in a central prototypical instance and resemblance relations between more peripheral instances and the central prototype (*see* FAMILY RESEMBLANCE). To illustrate, the concept of a bird has as its central prototype a bird such as a sparrow, and other entities that are not sparrows count as birds in virtue of their resemblances to sparrows. Thus may penguins and ostriches count as more peripheral instances of birdhood.

qualia, phenomenal properties; properties of conscious experiences (*see* EXPERIENCE) in virtue of which there is something it is like to have experiences (*see* WHAT IT IS LIKE). Some philosophers have favored relatively demanding definitions of qualia. Such definitions go beyond simply defining qualia as the properties of experience in virtue of which there is something it is like to have experience. These definitions add one or more of the following elements to the definition of qualia: (1) that qualia are intrinsic, nonrelational, properties (thus making the existence of qualia inconsistent with FUNCTIONAL-ISM); (2) that qualia lack intentionality (thus ruling out the possible truth of representational theories of qualia such as FIRST-ORDER REPRESENTATIONALISM and the HIGHER-ORDER-THOUGHT THEORY OF CONSCIOUSNESS); and (3) that possessors of qualia enjoy especially strong forms of FIRST-PERSON AUTHORITY with respect to qualia (thus rendering highly problematic if not impossible any theory of qualia consistent with NATURALISM). Discussions of qualia have played central roles in the development of various challenges to PHYSICALISM. For further discussion of such challenges, *see* KNOWLEDGE ARGUMENT; INVERTED SPECTRUM; MODAL ARGUMENT; ZOMBIE.

qualities, properties. *See* PROPERTY. *See also* PRIMARY QUALITIES; SECONDARY QUALITIES.

quantifying in, due to W.V.O. QUINE, a phrase describing sentences that involve a quantifier occurring outside of an opaque context binding a variable occurring inside of an opaque context (*see* OPACITY, REFERENTIAL; INTENSION (WITH AN "S"); INTENSIONALITY). ("Quantifying in" may be regarded as short for "quantifying into an opaque context.") Examples include (but are not limited to) certain kinds of belief attribution and certain kinds of quotation. To illustrate, consider,

1. There is someone such that Ralph believes that he is a spy.
2. There is someone such that Ralph said, "He is a spy."

which involve quantifying in, and

3. There is someone such that Ralph threw a ball to him.

which does not.

Quine held quantifying in to be deeply problematic. The problem is especially clear in cases such as (2). In (2), the word "He" does not refer to some male person of whom anything is being predicated. Here, the word "He," occurring inside of quotation marks, refers to the first word in Ralph's four-word utterance. Contrast (2) with (3) wherein "him" refers to a male person to whom Ralph threw a ball. Quine held attributions of belief such as (1) to involve quantifying in and thus be more similar to sentences like (2) than to sentences like (3).

radical translation, a (perhaps hypothetical) activity, discussed by W.V.O. QUINE, in which one attempts to translate an alien language into one's own language without the benefit of assistance from bilinguals. Quine held that any such translation was undetermined by all available evidence and that multiple translations could equally fit the evidence while disagreeing with one another. *See also* INDETERMINACY OF TRANSLATION; INSCRUTABILITY OF REFERENCE.

Ramsey sentence, due to Frank Ramsey, a sentence wherein the content of a theory is restated as a multiply-general existentially-quantified conjunction—that is, a single sentence whose form is along the lines of "There exists an *x* and there exists a *y* and there exists a *z* . . . such that *x* is red and *x* is taller than *y* and *x* is touching *z* . . ." Ramsey sentences have been especially interesting to philosophers of mind because they provide a means of articulating FUNCTIONALISM in terms of functional definitions of mental-state terms expressed as Ramsey sentences. The basic idea of functionalism is that a mental state of a creature may be defined in terms of the relations that state bears to the creature's inputs, outputs, and other mental states. Ramsey-sentence functionalism is a version of functionalism that articulates functional definitions in the form of Ramsey sentences. Such formulations are appealing, since they allow for a way of showing that the commitment of functionalism to the interdefinability of various mental terms does not commit functionalism to intolerably circular definitions.

Ramsification, the construction of a theory's RAMSEY SENTENCE.

rationalism, a view traditionally opposed to EMPIRICISM and that may be characterized as the view that at least one thing is in the mind without first being in the senses or, less sloganistically, as the view that at least some KNOWLEDGE has at least some of its justification by means other than sensory PERCEPTION and at least some of the things we meaningfully conceive of need not be perceived (or perhaps even perceivable) by the senses.

rationality, the capacity to engage in REASONING.

realism, in its global form, the view whereby everything that exists does so mind-independently—that is, each thing existing independent of anyone's saying or thinking that it exists. In its various local forms, realism involves

affirming the mind-independent existence of some restricted domain of entities. Thus, for example, to hold that the posits of FOLK PSYCHOLOGY (states such
as BELIEF and DESIRE) are more than mere useful fictions and have an existence
independent of anyone's finding it useful to say or think there are such things
is to hold a form of realism about such states. Realism, in general, is opposed
to two kinds of theory. The first kind is made up of versions of IDEALISM. The
second kind is made up of versions of *nihilism*. Where versions of realism
assert the mind-independent existence of something, versions of idealism
deny the *mind-independence* (while affirming the existence), and versions
of nihilism deny the existence of the things in question.

One way in which discussions of realism have been important to philosophy
of mind is with respect to debates concerning the ontological status of the
objects and properties of PERCEPTION. In connection with such issues, especially
as concern the objects of perception, *see* REPRESENTATIVE REALISM and DIRECT REALISM.
Regarding whether the properties that objects are perceived as having admit
of realistic treatment, *see* PRIMARY QUALITIES; SECONDARY QUALITIES; COLOR, THEORIES OF.

Another way in which discussions of realism have been important to philosophy of mind is with respect to debates concerning the ontological status of
mental states themselves. That people have mental states such as PROPOSITIONAL
ATTITUDES independently of whether anyone thinks or says that they have
mental states is part of a relatively robust form of realism about mental states
defended by philosophers such as Jerry FODOR. Various defenders of ELIMINATIVE
MATERIALISM have sought to deny the existence of such mental states. Thus is
eliminative materialism a kind of nihilism. One intermediate position between
eliminative materialism and robust realism is due to Daniel DENNETT, who affirms
that mental states such as propositional attitudes are those that are useful
for the prediction and EXPLANATION of human behavior when that behavior is
viewed from the INTENTIONAL STANCE.

reality, the sum total of the way things are, especially as contrasted with
the way things merely *appear* to be (*see* APPEARANCE). Standard philosophical
positions concerning reality hold that its independence of appearance involves
(1) that appearances do not logically determine reality—that is, it is always
possible that the way things appear is contrary to the way things really are,
and (2) reality can outstrip appearance in the sense that there can be more to
reality than can ever register in appearance. For instance, reality may contain

elements too fine or too remote to ever affect the realm of appearance. Points (1) and (2) help to characterize what is involved in the OBJECTIVITY of reality.

Some philosophers of mind have been concerned to point out that the above sort of characterization of reality as containing only objective reality is incomplete, as it leaves out an account of elements of reality that are inherently subjective (see SUBJECTIVITY). One strand of this line of thought asserts the reality of QUALIA as a kind of entity that is at once an appearance and has its reality exhausted by its appearance. For example, some have held that there's nothing more to the painfulness of PAIN than its seeming painful.

realization, of a (typically mental) PROPERTY, STATE, or EVENT, M, a minimal set of conditions, R, that jointly noncausally suffice to implement or bring about M. R realizes M. R is M's realization. If R_1 and R_2 are distinct realizations of M, then M is "multiply realized." The notion of realization plays a key role in discussions of MULTIPLE REALIZABILITY and FUNCTIONALISM. The elements of the definition of "realization" provided here help clarify this role. In particular, the inclusion of terms concerning "a minimal set of conditions" serves to differentiate cases in which there are multiple realizations from cases in which there is a single realization. If a proper subset of a set of jointly sufficient conditions for M is itself a set of jointly sufficient conditions for M, then the set and its proper subset do not count as multiple realizations of M. To illustrate, if having c-fibers fire suffices for having PAIN and having c-fibers fire while wearing a wool hat also suffices for having pain, then c-fibers with hat and c-fibers without hat do not count as two distinct realizations of having pain. The inclusion of terms specifying that the sufficient conditions in question noncausally suffice serves to distinguish the realization of M from whatever it is that is the cause of M. One way of viewing the distinction between realization and causation is that causes precede their effects but realizers are coinstantiated with what they realize. *See also* SUPERVENIENCE.

reasoning, the activity of entertaining REASONS. Alternately, COMPUTATION or figuring things out. Alternately, the sequences of mental events constitutive of RATIONALITY.

reasons, mental states capable of playing the dual roles of *causing* and *rationalizing* (rationally justifying) behaviors as well as other mental states.

There are, thus, reasons for action and reasons for belief. When George opens the refrigerator, his BELIEF that there is beer in the refrigerator conjoined with his DESIRE to drink beer not only constitutes the efficient *cause* of his opening the refrigerator, but the belief-desire pair also makes the opening of the refrigerator a rational ACTION. To illustrate reasons for belief instead of reasons for action, consider the reasons George may have for believing that there is beer in the refrigerator. Such reasons may be constituted by a MEMORY that he put beer in the refrigerator an hour ago and a perceptual belief that he's seen no one remove beer from the refrigerator in the intervening time. *See also* RATIONALITY.

On an alternate conception of reasons for action and reasons for belief, reasons are not thought of as mental states of a person, but objective norms (*see* OBJECTIVITY; NORMATIVE) concerning how they ought to act or what they ought to believe. Thus, if cigarette smoke causes cancer, then this fact is a reason why George should avoid smoking, regardless of whether George believes this fact or desires to avoid cancer. And this fact concerning the causes of cancer constitutes a reason for believing that George is likely to get cancer if he continues smoking, regardless of whether George is aware of or grasps this reason.

reduction, a relation between theories whereby one theory (the reduced theory) is derivable from either another theory (the reducing theory) or the reducing theory conjoined with one or more *bridging principles*. Bridging principles are required for specifying definitions of vocabulary from the reduced theory stated in vocabulary from the reducing theory. Thus is the theory of the relations between temperature and pressure in a sample of gas reduced to the theory of the kinematics of a collection of molecules. Derivatively, entities referred to in one theory are reduced to entities referred to in another if the aforementioned intertheoretic derivation relations hold. Thus may gasses be said to reduce to collections of molecules.

Contemporary philosophers of mind are interested in reduction insofar as it may be connected to the MIND-BODY PROBLEM via questions concerning whether psychological theories (including FOLK PSYCHOLOGY) or psychological entities reduce to physical theories or entities. *See also* PHYSICALISM, REDUCTIVE.

In the early part of the twentieth century, the main kind of reductionism discussed was not the reduction of the mental to the physical, but proposed reductions of physical objects to statements concerning SENSE-DATA. *See* PHENO-MENALISM; LOGICAL POSITIVISM; SENSE-DATUM THEORY. Influential criticisms of this sort of reductionism were due to W.V.O. QUINE and Wilfrid SELLARS.

reference, the designation or denotation of an entity (the referent) by a term or symbol (the thing that refers). In the study of SEMANTICS, reference is often contrasted with SENSE.

reference, direct, *see* DIRECT REFERENCE.

representation, an entity bearing INTENTIONALITY or CONTENT. Alternately, the bearing of intentionality or content by such an entity or by a person in virtue of possessing such an entity. While philosophers of mind are more interested in the notion of MENTAL REPRESENTATION than in the general notion of representation that applies to both mental and nonmental representations, some philosophers of mind have been interested in the question of whether nonmental representations have their content or intentionality only derivatively in virtue of relations borne to mental representations. One possible position is to hold, for example, that a nonmental representation such as a sign with the words "Beware of Dog" on it has its intentionality only derivatively insofar as a community of language-users interprets the sign in certain ways. It is consistent to hold additionally that mental states themselves have nonderived intentionality and, unlike the "Beware of Dog" sign, do not depend on being interpreted. Such a view—that mental states have nonderived intentionality—is defended by John SEARLE. Daniel DENNETT defends an opposing view: that all intentionality is derived intentionality.

representative realism, a theory of PERCEPTION that holds, in opposition to IDEALISM and PHENOMENALISM and in agreement with DIRECT REALISM, that *what* we perceive—the *object of perception*—exists independently of our perceiving it and, in opposition to direct realism, that *how* we perceive is via either a conscious or unconscious INFERENCE that begins with the direct awareness of a MENTAL REPRESENTATION and ends by hypothesizing the existence of a mind-independent entity.

One of the main advantages of representative realism is the relative ease with which it accounts for an apparent similarity between accurate perceptions of real objects on the one hand and, on the other hand, hallucinations, dreams, and illusory perceptions. If a hallucination of an elephant can be subjectively indistinguishable from the accurate perception of an elephant, and it makes sense to posit a mental-representational object of AWARENESS in the hallucination case, then it seems inviting to posit a mental-representational object for the accurate perceptual case as well—an object that serves as an intermediary between the perceiver and the real elephant.

One of the main disadvantages of representative realism is that it has seemed to many of its critics to give rise to an intolerable SKEPTICISM whereby external REALITY, if a mere posit based on direct awareness of a mental intermediary, is not really knowable since it is always possible that the inference to such a reality is erroneous. *See also* SKEPTICAL HYPOTHESIS.

res cogitans, from the philosophy of René DESCARTES, a thinking thing or a thinking SUBSTANCE. *See also* COGITO; DUALISM, SUBSTANCE.

res extensa, from the philosophy of René DESCARTES, an extended thing or an extended SUBSTANCE. *See* EXTENSION. *See also* DUALISM, SUBSTANCE.

resemblance theory of content, an attempt to explain the INTENTIONALITY or CONTENT of a mental state in terms of some resemblance that the state bears to other things. Some versions of the resemblance theory of content rely on first-order resemblances: A first-order resemblance obtains between two things in virtue of the two things having the same PROPERTY. Thus may a red apple bear a first-order resemblance to a red tomato. It's difficult, however, to see how states of a person can bear first-order resemblances to the objects the person is capable of thinking about, since states of objects are quite different entities from objects themselves. For example, while a person may be six feet tall and objects thought about by the person may be six feet tall, it makes little sense to say that any STATE of a person has a height, be it six feet or other. Thus, many versions of the resemblance theory of content rely on second-order or higher-order resemblances between states of persons and other things. To illustrate higher-order resemblances, a tone and a color may not bear a first-order resemblance to each other, but tones may be ordered with respect to their pitch and colors ordered with respect to their brightness, and the pattern of pitch orderings of tones resembles the pattern of brightness orderings of colors. Via such a scheme of higher-order resemblances, a high-pitched tone may be utilized to represent a bright color. Via an analogous scheme of higher-order resemblances, the pattern of similarities and differences between mental states may resemble the pattern of similarities and differences between environmental objects and thus may mental states *represent* environmental objects, according to certain versions of the resemblance theory of content.

robot, a machine capable of motion through an environment with such motion under the control of one or more of the following three kinds of mechanical components: (1) sensors for collecting INFORMATION from the environment, (2) a memory in which a program may be stored that determines behavioral responses as well as data collected from sensors, and (3) a processing unit capable of performing COMPUTATION by operating on information from either the sensors or the MEMORY. Philosophers of mind have been interested in discussing the possibility of robots that are as behaviorally complex and exhibit as much INTELLIGENCE as adult human beings. *See also* ARTIFICIAL INTELLIGENCE; FUNCTIONALISM; MULTIPLE REALIZABILITY.

role theory of content, (*see also* USE THEORY OF MEANING) also known as "inferential-role theory of content," "conceptual-role theory of content," and "functional-role theory of content," an attempt to explain the INTENTIONALITY or CONTENT of a mental state largely, if not exclusively, in terms of relations the mental state enters into with other mental states. Alternately, an application of FUNCTIONALISM to the problem of intentionality. Role theories are especially plausible as accounts of the meanings of logical connectives. It is plausible that there is nothing more to the meaning of "and" beyond the role it plays in certain inferences. Among the main worries about role theories is one that concerns how it is that intra-mental relations between, for example, the mental symbol "rock" and other mental entities can constitute one's thinking about rocks, which, since no one literally has rocks in their heads, are extra-mental entities. Versions of role theories known as "two-factor theories" postulate a second factor involving relations to extra-mental items. *See also* CONCEPTUAL-ROLE SEMANTICS.

Sapir–Whorf hypothesis, a thesis of LINGUISTIC DETERMINISM named after Edward Sapir (1884–1939) and Benjamin Lee Whorf (1897–1941).

scientific realism, a version of REALISM concerned specifically with affirming the existence of the entities posited by scientific theories, and further, that such entities exist regardless of whether they are observable and exist independently of our theories about them. Scientific realism is traditionally opposed to the views of scientific entities expressed in INSTRUMENTALISM and LOGICAL POSITIVISM. One of the main lines of reasoning in support of scientific realism is that if the entities posited by scientific theories did not exist, then the predictive and explanatory successes of science would themselves be unexplained miracles. That scientific realism is true is posited to explain why science works as well as it does. *See also* OBJECTIVITY; PHENOMENALISM; EXPLANATION.

secondary qualities, a kind of property of material objects, distinguished by John LOCKE from PRIMARY QUALITIES and characterized by reference to dispositions or powers to cause certain sensory responses in perceivers (*see* SENSATION). Typical examples of secondary qualities include the color, temperature, and odor of a material object.

seeing, visual perceiving (*see* PERCEPTION). The philosopher Fred DRETSKE argued for a distinction between two kinds of seeing (and by extension, two kinds of perceiving): epistemic seeing and nonepistemic seeing. In epistemic seeing, what one sees is always of the form *that* such-and-such is the case: for instance, one sees that *the door is open* or that *some dogs are in the yard*. Epistemic seeing is thus a kind of PROPOSITIONAL ATTITUDE. According to Dretske, seeing is believing when the seeing involved is epistemic seeing. Thus, it is a requirement on seeing, for instance, that a dog is in the room that one thereby have the BELIEF that a dog is in the room, which in turn requires the possession of CONCEPTS such as the concept of dogs and the concept of rooms. In contrast, no such requirements hold of nonepistemic seeing. As long as one is in an appropriate causal relation (mediated, for example, by mechanisms for the transduction of light) with an object, one may nonepistemically see that object without there being some particular belief or concept that must be applied to that object. Thus, for example, a newborn baby who has not yet acquired the concept of a dog may nonetheless see a dog that moves through the baby's field of view. *See also* NONCONCEPTUAL CONTENT.

seeing, epistemic, *see* SEEING.

seeing, nonepistemic, *see* SEEING.

self, the, an alleged entity, belonging to each person and constituting that person's essence or identity (*see* PERSONAL IDENTITY). Alternately, that which is referred to (*see* REFERENCE) by use of FIRST-PERSON pronouns. Philosophical views vary widely on the existence and nature of selves, ranging from René DESCARTES's view that selves are nonmaterial thinking substances (*see* SUBSTANCE) to David HUME's view that there are no such things as selves.

self-consciousness, an AWARENESS of oneself, an awareness *of* the self *by* the self (*see* SELF, THE). It is often thought that a special faculty, namely INTROSPECTION, mediates self-consciousness. Some philosophers have held that the KNOWLEDGE yielded by such a faculty enjoys a special status. They have held that, for example, it constitutes an especially *certain* form of knowledge. *See* FIRST-PERSON AUTHORITY. *See also* KNOWLEDGE BY ACQUAINTANCE.

Some philosophers have held that all CONSCIOUSNESS is self-consciousness. René DESCARTES held that all of one's mental states are states of which one is aware. Immanuel KANT held that all of one's representations (*see* MENTAL REPRESENTATION) must be able to be accompanied by a thought of the form "I think." Related to the view that all consciousness is self-consciousness is the view, central to the HIGHER-ORDER-THOUGHT THEORY OF CONSCIOUSNESS, that in order for one's mental state to be a conscious state (*see* CONSCIOUSNESS, STATE), one must be conscious *of* that mental state. Other philosophers have denied that all consciousness is self-consciousness. Related to this view is the thesis of the TRANSPARENCY (OF EXPERIENCE), according to which one's conscious states make one conscious of, for instance, external REALITY but not conscious of experiences themselves.

self-control, *see* WEAKNESS OF WILL.

self-deception, the process of either intentionally or unintentionally (*see* INTENTION) instilling in oneself a BELIEF that is false. Self-deception is both something that is quite common and philosophically deeply perplexing. Regarding how common self-deception is, consider how often we encounter, in ourselves or others, instances of wishful thinking or being in a "state of denial." One source of perplexity arises if we assume both that the process of self-deception is done consciously and that conscious states are states of which we are aware (*see* SELF-CONSCIOUSNESS). If I am to deliberately instill a false belief in myself, it would seem on these prior assumptions that I have a prior belief that it is false, and thus, I believe its negation. Successfully intentionally arriving at this false belief would seem to involve winding up with a contradictory set of beliefs. One sort of solution to this puzzle is to hold, as Sigmund Freud did, that the processes of self-deception are unconscious (*see* UNCONSCIOUS, THE). Another source of perplexity is that the idea of intentionally changing one's belief runs afoul of the widespread idea that beliefs are not the sort of thing upon which we may exert direct control. However, there are philosophers who defend a variety of *voluntarism*, known as DOXASTIC voluntarism, whereby beliefs may come under the direct control of the will. *See* WILL, THE. *See also* WEAKNESS OF WILL.

self-presenting, the alleged property of a THOUGHT of being about (*see* INTENTIONALITY), among other things, itself. Some philosophers have claimed all thought to be self-presenting. If this is so, then the thought that *grass is green* is not simply about grass or about the STATE OF AFFAIRS of grass's being green, but the thought is also about the thought itself. *See also* SELF-CONSCIOUSNESS.

self-reproducing automaton, a machine capable of making copies of itself. In the early part of the twentieth century, the early computer scientist John von Neumann presented an abstract proof of the possibility of such an automaton. The proof involved demonstrating the possibility of a universal constructor. Being universal, it could construct anything, including copies of itself. *See also* ROBOT; ARTIFICIAL INTELLIGENCE.

semantics, the study of meaning and significance, which includes the study of such things as CONTENT; SENSE; REFERENCE; TRUTH; EXTENSION (1); INTENSION (WITH AN "S"). Alternately, the entities and properties thereby studied. *See also* CONCEPTUAL-ROLE SEMANTICS.

sensation, an allegedly preconceptual conscious state that figures among the raw materials out of which a PERCEPTION may be formed. Thus, for example, one may contrast a *sensation* of red and a *perception* of a red apple. Some philosophers hold that a perception of a red apple involves the application of CONCEPTS such as the concept of redness and the concept of being an apple (see SEEING, EPISTEMIC). But the *sensation* of redness is a causal intermediary between the red apple itself and the triggering of the application of the relevant concepts.

One puzzling feature of sensations is their INTENSIONALITY. One illustration of the intensionality of sensation, pointed out by Wilfrid SELLARS, is that one can have a red sensation, as when one sees a red afterimage, even though no existing red object is currently present in your immediate environment. Further, all red objects may cease to exist, but it would still be possible for one to undergo a *sensation* of redness. Another illustration of the intensionality of sensation, pointed out by Michael Tye, is that if one had a sensation of PAIN in one's finger and placed one's finger in one's mouth, one would not thereby have a pain in one's mouth. Some philosophers have attempted to reduce the intensionality of sensation to the intensionality of MENTAL REPRESENTATION by arguing that sensations themselves have INTENTIONALITY. Such a view has been held by defenders of FIRST-ORDER REPRESENTATIONALISM such as Tye and Fred DRETSKE. See also QUALIA; NONCONCEPTUAL CONTENT.

sensationalism, the theory that all mental states, including states of MEMORY and BELIEF, either are, or are composed of, sensations (see SENSATION). An early expression of sensationalism was due to the philosopher Thomas Hobbes, who wrote, "There is no conception in man's mind which has not at first, totally, or by parts, been begotten upon the organs of sense. The rest are derived from that original." See also EMPIRICISM.

sense, in contrast with REFERENCE, the connotation (as opposed to the denotation) of a term or symbol. Alternately, the *mode of presentation* of a referent. While "Venus" and "second planet from the sun" share a referent, they diverge with respect to their sense or way in which they present what it is that they refer to. An influential line of thought concerning sense is due to Gottlob Frege. On Frege's view, the existence of senses or modes of presentation must be posited to account for the difference in cognitive significance or informativeness between identity statements such as (1) "Venus is Venus" and (2) "Venus is the second planet from the sun." Arguably, (1) is uninformative and knowable a priori whereas (2) is informative and knowable only a posteriori. If, however, there were nothing more to the cognitive significance of a referring term than the entity that the term refers to (*see* DIRECT REFERENCE), then the differences highlighted between (1) and (2) would be exceedingly difficult to account for. *See also* SEMANTICS; INTENSION (WITH AN "S"); INTENSIONALITY.

sense data, plural for *sense datum*, the mental intermediaries postulated by theories of PERCEPTION such as versions of REPRESENTATIVE REALISM like the SENSE-DATUM THEORY, and held by some theories, such as PHENOMENALISM, to be the ultimate basis of all existing things in that so-called physical objects are mere logical constructions out of sense data. The properties of sense data are QUALIA. *See also* LOGICAL POSITIVISM; ARGUMENT FROM ILLUSION.

sense-datum theory, the theory that what we have direct knowledge of are mind-dependent entities known as SENSE DATA. *See also* PHENOMENALISM.

sensibilia, plural for "sensible," a term used by Bertrand Russell for items of which no one is currently aware but are in all other respects just like the items of which one is directly aware in undergoing sensory PERCEPTION. If one adopts a theory of DIRECT REALISM, then sensibilia just are ordinary mind-independent objects. If, however, one does not adopt direct realism, then the existence of sensibilia is highly problematic, for it is difficult, if not impossible, to see how items such as SENSE DATA, whose existence seem to be exhausted by one's direct awareness of them, can exist independently of such awareness.

sensibles, common, from the philosophy of ARISTOTLE, properties such as size, shape, and motion, which may be perceived by multiple sensory modalities—for example, touch and vision. In contrast are *special sensibles,* such as colors and flavors, which may each be perceived by only a single sensory modality—for example, sight for colors and taste for flavors. The properties sorted by Aristotle into the common sensibles and the special sensibles roughly correspond to John LOCKE'S distinction between PRIMARY QUALITIES and SECONDARY QUALITIES.

sensorium, the basis, in humans and animals, for PERCEPTION and SENSATION.

simulation theory (theory of mind), in THEORY OF MIND, an account wherein a person represents another person's mental states by simulating them—that is, by entering into such states oneself. The simulation theory is oft contrasted with the "THEORY"-THEORY (THEORY OF MIND).

skeptical hypothesis, a proposition that, if believed by some subject, would undermine that subject's BELIEF or degree of certainty in some other proposition. For example, if I believed that I was recently given a hallucinogenic drug, then that belief would undermine my degree of certainty concerning the current color of the sky right now. I currently believe that the sky is blue right now, but if I believed that there was a good chance that I was hallucinating, I would be less certain about whether the sky *really was* blue right now (and not gray and overcast). Some philosophers have held that a belief cannot count as KNOWLEDGE unless potentially undermining skeptical hypotheses can be ruled out. For example, my current belief that I am reading words on a printed page cannot count as knowledge unless I can rule out the possibility that I am really dreaming this or being deceived by a demon. *See also* SKEPTICISM; BRAIN IN A VAT.

skepticism, in its practical form (practical skepticism), an attitude of withholding belief about some class of propositions, and in its theoretical form (theoretical skepticism), the view that there cannot be KNOWLEDGE concerning some class of propositions. One especially influential and widely discussed form of theoretical skepticism concerns skepticism about the external world and the question of whether the failure to rule out a SKEPTICAL HYPOTHESIS such as the possibility that I am dreaming or that I am a BRAIN IN A VAT undermines all of my claims to have empirical knowledge of a world external to my mind. Another form of skepticism, and one especially pertinent to the philosophy of mind, is skepticism about other minds. *See* OTHER MINDS, PROBLEM OF.

slow switching, a hypothetical process whereby a thinker's WIDE CONTENT changes as a result of being in a new context for a while. For example, some proponents of EXTERNALISM propose that if an Earthling were transported to TWIN EARTH, the CONTENT of certain of their CONCEPTS, such as the concept expressible by utterances of the word "water," would, after some time, switch from being about H_2O to being about XYZ. Slow switching is slow in comparison to the quick switching that accompanies certain INDEXICAL representations such as "here," which has a different wide content immediately upon moving to a distinct location.

solipsism, the view that the only entity in existence is one's own self (*see* SELF, THE). Solipsism is typically discussed in philosophy not because it has many advocates (if one *were* a solipsist, why bother attempting to convince anyone else?) but instead because it has been an interesting problem to demonstrate how it is that, if it *is* false, it can be *known* to be false. It is worth noting the distinction between, on the one hand, solipsism and, on the other hand, SKEPTICISM about the external world. Solipsism is the denial of the existence of a world external to one's own mind. In contrast, external-world skepticism is a denial that it can be *known* whether there is a world external to one's own mind. The truth of external-world skepticism, but not the truth of solipsism, is consistent with there actually being an external world.

split brain, a colloquial term for the result of a commissurotomy, a surgical procedure that severs connections between the right and left cerebral hemi-spheres, especially connections between the hemispheres mediated by the brain structure known as the *corpus callosum*. Such surgical procedures are used for the treatment of especially severe cases of epilepsy. Several interest-ing observations have been made about split-brain patients. Such observations indicate high degrees of specialization in the cerebral hemispheres, with, for example, right-handed patients having their left hemispheres be the predomi-nant seat of language-related functions. One kind of supporting observation for this thesis is that a (right-handed) split-brain patient can name an object placed in his or her right hand but not placed in his or her left hand. It is thought that the left hemisphere is largely responsible for the right side of the body and the right hemisphere for the left. Thus, the above-described observation seems to indicate that tactile INFORMATION about object identity can reach language centers in the left hemisphere only if transduced by sensory receptors on the right side of the body (such as in the right hand).

state, the INSTANTIATION of a PROPERTY by an object at a time. The condition of an object or system at a time. The way an object or system is at a time.

The kinds of states that have been of most central concern to philosophers of mind are states of persons, in particular mental states such as PROPOSITIONAL ATTITUDES (paradigmatic examples being states of BELIEF and states of DESIRE) and SENSATIONS. *See also* PAIN; EMOTION; PERCEPTION; INTROSPECTION; VOLITION; THOUGHT. Per-sons are typically taken to have, in addition to their mental states, states that may be characterized as being physical states, states such as the state of weighing two hundred pounds or the state of having one's c-fibers fire. One way of characterizing the central problem in the philosophy of mind, the

MIND/BODY PROBLEM, is as the problem concerning the relation mental states bear to physical states of persons. Related issues concern whether the mental states of persons depend on a person bearing relations to entities in his or her external environment (including other persons). Proponents of EXTERNALISM affirm such an environmental dependence of mental states. Proponents of INTERNALISM deny it.

state of affairs, the actual, possible, or impossible entities named by nominalizations of declarative sentences. For example, the declarative sentence "This book is authored by Pete Mandik" can be nominalized either as "this book's being authored by Pete Mandik" or "that this book is authored by Pete Mandik." In the above example, an actual state of affairs is named by the resulting nominalizations. An example of an impossible state of affairs would be this book's being written by someone who is not identical to himself. One reason philosophers have been interested in states of affairs is to utilize them in giving an account of TRUTH. For example, according to a version of the *correspondence theory of truth,* a *truth bearer* (something that can have a truth value—that is, can be either true or false), such as a PROPOSITION, BELIEF, or sentence—is true if and only if it bears a relation of correspondence to a *truth maker*, such as a fact or state of affairs. For example, the sentence "Mandik wrote a book" is true if and only if the sentence bears a correspondence relation to the state of affairs of Mandik writing a book.

subdoxastic, pertaining to mental states that are not themselves states of BELIEF, but are causal precursors to apparently noninferential beliefs. Like beliefs, subdoxastic states may have INTENTIONALITY or representational CONTENT (especially NONCONCEPTUAL CONTENT). But unlike beliefs, they are not accessible to INTROSPECTION and may not be available to partake in the wide range of inferences (*see* INFERENCE) that a belief can. To illustrate, my belief that there is a yellow book on the table is the causal consequence of various psychological or neurophysiological mechanisms that work on INFORMATION coming in through my eyes and perform various instances of COMPUTATION, none of which I have any kind of introspective access to. For example, while I may be able to directly introspect the presence of my belief that there is a yellow book on the table, I do not have direct introspective access to the transduction of light of such-and-such frequency by such-and-such neurons in my retina. *See also* SUB-PERSONAL; DOXASTIC.

subjectivity, (1) Of that which exists, that its existence depends on some-one's PERCEPTION of it or THOUGHT or BELIEF about it. (2) Of that which exists, KNOWLEDGE about it being acquirable via limited kinds of EXPERIENCE. (3) Of mental states, especially judgments or beliefs, that they fail to be impartial and instead reflect the bias of the judge or believer and have their TRUTH value (true or false) in virtue of factors that have subjectivity in sense (1) of the term. All three senses of "subjectivity" may be contrasted against correlative senses of OBJECTIVITY. For further discussion of both subjectivity and objectivity, see the entry on objectivity.

sub-personal, due to Daniel DENNETT, a term denoting a level of EXPLANATION below the level that involves the mental states of a person and involves instead mechanical explanations in terms of brain states. The sub-personal level is the level below the level that is "seen" from the INTENTIONAL STANCE: the personal level. While the personal level is discernable from the intentional stance, the sub-personal level is discernable from the physical stance and the design stance. The sub-personal level is an explanatory level that involves states of and events in a person's nervous system. The personal level is an explanatory level that involves mental states such as PROPOSITIONAL ATTITUDES (such as states of BELIEF and DESIRE) and states of SENSATION. The personal level also involves seeing a person as an AGENT capable of exhibiting RATIONALITY. *See also* SUBDOXASTIC.

subsistence, from the philosophy of Meinong, the kind of being possessed by abstract entities such as those studied by mathematics and distinguished from *existence*, the kind of being possessed by physical objects. Thus, while rocks and rivers *exist*, the square root of two and the set of prime numbers *subsist*. Meinong held that being was not exhausted by existence and sub-sistence, since mental states with INTENTIONALITY could have as their intentional objects entities that neither exist nor subsist, such as when one thinks about an impossible concrete state of affairs. For example, if one were to have a thought about a stone cylinder that had a diameter greater than its circumfer-ence—being stone, it does not *subsist* and being impossible (since a round object's diameter cannot exceed its circumference), it does not *exist*. *See also* INEXISTENCE.

substance, something that may exist independently of other things while other things may depend upon it. For example, the properties (*see* PROPERTY) of a substance may depend on the substance insofar as those property instances would cease to exist if the substance ceased existing. If my blue coffee mug ceased to exist, that particular instance of blueness would likewise cease existing. However, a substance may continue existing despite changing its properties. If my blue coffee mug were painted red, it may still be one and the same substance that simply endured a change in color. Some philosophers, such as John LOCKE, hold substances to be the part of an object in which the object's properties inhere. Thus the color and shape of the coffee mug inhere in the substance of the coffee mug. Other philosophers, such as David HUME, deny the existence of substances, holding instead that objects are bundles of properties with no distinct part, the substance, in which the properties inhere. Thus, there is nothing more to the coffee mug than its shape, its color, its solidity, its translucency, and so on.

supervenience, a determination relation that holds between sets of proper-ties and typically claimed of the set, P, of physical properties and the set, M, of mental properties, wherein there can be no differences (between objects at a time or within objects over time) with respect to M properties without there being differences (between objects at a time or within objects over time) with respect to P properties. It is left open whether this holds in the opposite direction and thus is supervenience consistent with both reductive and non-reductive versions of PHYSICALISM (*see* PHYSICALISM, REDUCTIVE; PHYSICALISM, NONREDUCTIVE). A typical sort of claim a philosopher of mind will make in terms of super-venience is to claim that a person's mental properties supervene upon a person's intrinsic physical properties (*see* INTERNALISM). One entailment of such a supervenience claim is that a person cannot change with respect to his or her mental properties without changing with respect to his or her intrinsic physical properties. Another entailment of such a supervenience claim is that two numerically distinct people cannot differ with respect to their mental properties without differing with respect to their intrinsic physical properties.

Swamp Man, a hypothetical being from a THOUGHT EXPERIMENT by Donald DAVIDSON, who (the hypothetical being) is maximally similar to a normal human being except for whatever is logically entailed by the fact that the being just popped into existence and thus, unlike the normal human it is otherwise similar to, Swamp Man completely lacks a history. Following Davidson's use of Swamp Man, the thought experiments of various other philosophers employ Swamp Man to probe intuitions (*see* INTUITION) concerning whether and to what degree the mental states of a being depend on the learning, developmental, and evolutionary history of that being. A Swamp Man that duplicates my intrinsic physical properties would have the same behavioral dispositions as I do and would make the same utterances I would make in response to the question, "What did you do April 17, 2008?" Namely, it would respond, for example, by uttering, "I wrote the first draft of an entry on Swamp Man." However, it is arguable that in spite of our intrinsic physical similarities, a Swamp Man that popped into existence after April 17, 2008, can't count as having *remembered* performing any actions on that date (*see* MEMORY). One cannot count as remembering something that didn't actually happen, and Swamp Man's state is, at best, a *quasi-memory*. Some philosophers, especially those attracted to certain versions of TELEOSE-MANTICS, argue that *none* of Swamp Man's states have any CONTENT or INTENTIONALITY. Some philosophers, especially those attracted to certain versions of FIRST-ORDER REPRESENTATIONALISM, argue that none or at least very few of Swamp Man's states are CONSCIOUS or have any QUALIA. According to an extreme form of this line of thought, Swamp Man is a ZOMBIE.

symbol grounding, a relation or process that bestows a REPRESENTATION (a symbol) with its representational CONTENT.

symbolicism, a school of thought regarding COGNITIVE ARCHITECTURE that holds that mental states and processes are implemented as rule-governed symbol manipulations (*see* COMPUTATION) in a LANGUAGE OF THOUGHT. Symbolicism is an approach often contrasted against both CONNECTIONISM and DYNAMIC SYSTEMS THEORY. Symbolicism is closely related to an approach to ARTIFICIAL INTELLIGENCE that John Haugeland has dubbed GOFAI (Good Old-Fashioned Artificial Intelligence).

syntax, oft contrasted with SEMANTICS, the properties of representational or linguistic items that concern the manipulation of and interactions between such items, especially those properties that are independent of the semantic properties (e.g., the TRUTH, REFERENCE, or SENSE) of such items. In linguistics, the syntax of a natural language is constituted by the rules or principles for the construction of sentences out of words. In logic and computer science, the syntax of formal systems such as logical calculi and programming languages is constituted by the rules governing the behavior of elements in such systems. One key role that the notion of syntax has played in the philosophy of mind has been in discussions of a hypothetical LANGUAGE OF THOUGHT whereby mental states (such as BELIEF) and processes (such as REASONING) are hypothesized to be governed by a mental syntax.

systematicity, one of the key properties exhibited by collections of thoughts (*see* THOUGHT) that, along with PRODUCTIVITY and COMPOSITIONALITY, Jerry FODOR appeals to in articulating and arguing for the LANGUAGE OF THOUGHT hypothesis. Systematicity is exhibited, for instance, by the thoughts of a person who is not only capable of thinking or understanding that *John kisses Mary* but is also capable of thinking or understanding that *Mary kisses John*. The claim of systematicity is thus that thinkers are capable of thinking thoughts that are systematically related to each other. The language-of-thought hypothesis is supposed to explain such systematicity in the following manner: The reason that any thinker capable of thinking *John kisses Mary* is also capable of thinking *Mary kisses John* is that the thought *John kisses Mary* has as parts a separate MENTAL REPRESENTATION each for John, Mary, and the kissing relation, respectively. Further, such representational parts are combinable in accordance with a mental SYNTAX that allows *Mary kisses John* as readily as it allows *John kisses Mary*.

teleology, purposiveness. Alternately, being forward-looking or conditioned by the future. According to some thinkers, hearts exhibit teleology insofar as they have the purpose of pumping blood, and this very book exhibits teleology insofar as it has the purpose of spreading knowledge about the philosophy of mind. A key feature of teleology is that something can have a purpose without fulfilling its purpose. For example, the eyes of a blind person can be *for* seeing even though they fail to *do* what they are for. For another example, an artifact can be *for* taking pictures even though, due to damage or poor design, or not yet having been used, the artifact is not currently taking pictures. On one account of teleology, especially well suited for accounting for the teleology of artifacts, is that the purpose of an item is bestowed by the INTENTION of its designer. For example, what makes some carved piece of wood a doorstop instead of a decorative bookend is that it was intended as such by its manufacturer. However, unless some supernatural creator exists, such an account is ill-suited for naturally occurring (not manmade) instances of teleology. On an alternate account of teleology, things that are not artifacts exhibit teleology in virtue of being products of evolution by natural selection. Thus, for example, what it means to say of hearts that they have the purpose of pumping blood is that hearts have, by pumping blood in previous generations, supplied a survival and reproductive advantage to creatures with blood-pumping hearts. Philosophers of mind have been interested in the way that appeals to teleology can ground key notions concerning the mind. For an ancient example, ARISTOTLE held that if the eye were an animal, then sight would be its soul. More recently, some philosophers of mind have advocated TELEOSEMANTICS, a research program attempting to ground INTENTIONALITY and CONTENT in terms of teleology, especially as explicated in terms of evolution by natural selection.

teleosemantics, an attempt to explain the INTENTIONALITY or CONTENT of a mental STATE in terms of TELEOLOGY—that is, in terms of what the *purpose* of the state is. On a popular version of teleosemantics, the purpose of a mental state is determined by the evolutionary history of the species to which belongs the individual having the mental states. One of the main appealing features of teleosemantics is that it offers a potential EXPLANATION of how *misrepresentation* is possible. A creature can misrepresent its environment as containing a red object even though there is no red object. The teleosemanticist suggests that this be regarded as crucially similar to how some aspect of a creature's anatomy, physiology, or behavior can be *for* the production of a state of affairs that it happens to fail to produce (as when, for example, a creature has eyes that are *for* seeing but is confined to an environment or damaged in such a way that prevents it from using its eyes to do what they are for). On one version of teleosemantics, a CAUSAL THEORY OF CONTENT is combined with an explication of teleology in terms of evolution by natural selection. For example, a mental state comes to have the representational content that a wolf is present if states of that kind being triggered in the presence of wolves has been survival-conducive to one's evolutionary ancestors. On such an account, a state comes to represent the presence of wolves by being the state of a mechanism that was naturally selected for being a wolf detector. On such an account, misrepresentation is possible because something can be naturally selected for being a wolf detector even though it does not detect wolves on every occasion. The wolf detector may thus misfire and mistakenly indicate the presence of a wolf even though no wolf is present. *See also* Ruth MILLIKAN.

theoretical term, a term in a scientific theory alleged or purported to refer (*see* REFERENCE) to an unobservable entity. Examples include "electron" and "radio wave." Such terms are contrasted with observational terms—terms referring to observable entities such as "dog," "tree," and "coffee mug." At the core of the conflict between SCIENTIFIC REALISM and INSTRUMENTALISM is that scientific realists affirm and instrumentalists deny that theoretical terms refer to actually existing entities. In the philosophy of mind, some have argued, following Wilfrid SELLARS, that commonsense terms for mental STATES such as states of BELIEF or SENSATION are actually theoretical terms (the embedding "scientific" theory being FOLK PSYCHOLOGY) as opposed to terms denoting enti- ties with which we have some kind of direct AWARENESS (*see* FIRST-PERSON AUTHORITY; KNOWLEDGE BY ACQUAINTANCE). Sellars, and more recent philosophers such as FODOR, advocate scientific realism about such mental-state terms. Instrumentalism about such terms has been defended by DENNETT, at least at certain points of his career. An extreme view concerning mental-state terms, defended by thinkers such as Paul and Patricia CHURCHLAND, is ELIMINATIVE MATERIALISM.

theory-laden, influenced by one's theoretical commitments. Being theory- laden is typically, though controversially, attributed to observations or perceptions (*see* PERCEPTION; PERCEPTUAL RELATIVITY). The claim that something is theory-laden is that what one perceives or how one perceives it (or alternately, the terminology with which one reports one's observations) reflects a bias toward the confirmation of an antecedently held theory. Insofar as observations are theory-laden, they seem to be ill-suited for neutral arbitration between competing theories. Part of FODOR's thesis of MODULARITY is that perceptual systems, being modular, are insulated against the effects of theories (theoretical commitments being held in nonmodular, central systems). Perceptual modules are thus "informationally encapsulated," according to Fodor. One kind of illustration of such informational encapsulation is the recalcitrance of certain perceptual illusions in the face of certain beliefs. For example, in the Müller-Lyer optical illusion, line segments of equal length appear unequal (due in part to the influence of differently oriented "arrow heads" at the segments' endpoints). Such an illusion may persist despite the observer's belief that the segments are, in reality, of equal length. Other philosophers of mind, notably Paul CHURCHLAND, have defended the idea of perception being theory-laden. *See also* LINGUISTIC DETERMINISM; SAPIR–WHORF HYPOTHESIS.

theory of mind, an ability to attribute mental states to other people as well as to oneself. Alternately, the ability to *understand* people including oneself in terms of mental states. Such understanding involves, among other things, the prediction and EXPLANATION of human ACTION by appeal to PROPOSITIONAL ATTITUDES such as BELIEF and DESIRE. For example, we may explain George's opening of the refrigerator by appeal to his belief that it has beer in it and his desire to drink beer. The phrase "theory of mind" is oft used to denote common-sense or everyday understanding of persons in terms of mental states. It is thus distinguishable from an explicitly scientific "theory of mind" as might be formulated in COGNITIVE SCIENCE. *See also* FOLK PSYCHOLOGY. The main accounts of what a person's grasp of theory of mind consists in include the simulation theory and the "theory"-theory. *See* SIMULATION THEORY (THEORY OF MIND); "THEORY"-THEORY (THEORY OF MIND).

"Theory"-theory (theory of mind), in debates concerning THEORY OF MIND, an account oft contrasted with the simulation theory (*see* SIMULATION THEORY (THEORY OF MIND)) that, unlike the simulation theory, explicates the understanding of oneself and others in terms of the application of a theory akin to the theories employed in the natural sciences (*see* SCIENTIFIC REALISM). *See also* FOLK PSYCHOLOGY.

thought, a kind of mental STATE—most broadly, any mental state with propositional CONTENT (*see* PROPOSITION; PROPOSITIONAL ATTITUDE). Less broadly, mental states with propositional content and distinguishable from states of PERCEPTION and EMOTION. Alternately, the process of undergoing such states; thinking (as in "she was lost in thought"). *See also* LANGUAGE OF THOUGHT.

A different use of "thought" is due to Gottlob Frege who held a thought to be not a mental state but, instead, a nonpsychological, objectively existing (*see* OBJECTIVITY) entity that serves as the SENSE of a sentence (the REFERENCE of a sentence being its TRUTH value).

thought experiment, a method for testing hypotheses by imagining certain scenarios and then arriving at judgments about what the outcomes of such scenarios would be, including, especially in philosophical thought experiments, how one would most intuitively describe the outcomes of such scenarios. Employment of philosophical thought experiments is a central method in the pursuit of CONCEPTUAL ANALYSIS. The use of thought experiments is not entirely uncontroversial. One sort of controversy surrounds the issue of whether CONCEIVABILITY entails or is at least a reliable guide to POSSIBILITY. It is difficult, however, to maintain an entirely dismissive attitude toward thought experiments, in part because some highly influential thought experiments have been employed in the natural sciences. For example, Einstein employed thought experiments in his arguments for the relativity of simultaneity, and Galileo employed thought experiments in his argument that objects of different mass nonetheless accelerate at the same rate in a given gravitational field. Examples of thought experiments that have received much attention in contemporary philosophy of mind include the thought experiments concerning SWAMP MAN; inverted QUALIA (*see* INVERTED SPECTRUM) and absent qualia (*see* ZOMBIE) (*see also* MODAL ARGUMENT); the color-blind super-neuroscientist, Mary, at the center of discussions of the KNOWLEDGE ARGUMENT; and the CHINESE ROOM and the CHINESE NATION thought experiment at the center of famous critiques of FUNCTIONALISM.

token, contrasted with TYPE, a *particular* or *unrepeatable* in contrast with a *universal* or *repeatable*. To illustrate, in "The boy fought with the other boy at the store" there are ten word tokens, two of which are tokens of the word type "boy" and three of which are tokens of the word type "the."

Altogether, seven word types are "tokened": "the," "boy," "fought," "with," "other," "at," and "store." The distinction between type and token has been especially useful to philosophers interested in utilizing this distinction to articulate various versions of PHYSICALISM—namely, the TYPE-IDENTITY THESIS and the TOKEN-IDENTITY THESIS. For example, a philosopher who affirms the type-identity thesis would hold that if two creatures were undergoing the same type of mental state, say PAIN, they must do so in virtue of undergoing the same type of physical state, say having c-fibers fire. Further, such a philosopher would hold that the mental type *pain* is identical to (one and the same as) the physical type *c-fibers firing*. For another example, a philosopher who denies the type-identity thesis but affirms the token-identity thesis may hold that two creatures can both be in pain, but the pain token in the one creature could be identical to a very different physical token than is the pain token in the other creature. For instance, the pain token in the first creature may be identical to a physical token of c-fibers firing and the pain token in the second creature may be identical to activity in a silicon-chip computer implant (the second creature being a synthetic creature [*see* ROBOT]). *See also* MULTIPLE REALIZABILITY.

token-identity thesis, (*see* PHYSICALISM, NONREDUCTIVE) a version of PHYSICALISM that is contrasted against the TYPE-IDENTITY THESIS version of physicalism by denying that mental types (*see* TYPE) are identical to physical types. The token-identity thesis is claimed to be a version of *physicalism* in virtue of claiming that all mental tokens (*see* TOKEN) are identical to physical tokens. For example, an adherent of the token-identity thesis may claim that each token of the mental type PAIN is identical to (one and the same as) a token of a physical type (such as c-fibers firing). It is open for adherents of the token-identity thesis to also affirm the type-identity thesis, but it is also open for them to deny it. Thus, if denying type identity, the adherent of token identity may hold, for example, that while each token of the mental type *pain* must be identical to some token of a physical type, various physical tokens that the various mental tokens are identical to need not all belong to the same physical type. One line of thought that leads some philosophers to affirm the token-identity thesis while denying the type-identity thesis is due to considerations hinging on MULTIPLE REALIZABILITY. Another line of thought leading to affirming the token-identity thesis while denying the type-identity thesis hinges on the thesis of ANOMALOUS MONISM developed by Donald DAVIDSON. Adherents of the token-identity thesis may make the additional claim that psychological properties supervene (see SUPERVENIENCE) on physical properties, as did Davidson.

topic-neutral, especially as pertains to descriptions or reports of states of persons, not committing one to any particular ontological or metaphysical position—for example, the metaphysical positions of DUALISM, PHYSICALISM, or IDEALISM. The philosopher J.J.C. Smart held that reports of INTROSPECTION such as "I am now having a red sensation" can be interpreted as noncommittal in the debate between, say, physicalists and dualists. So, for example, "I am now having a red sensation" might mean something equivalent to "I am in a state resembling the state I am in when I correctly visually perceive that an object is red" and need not commit me, the speaker, either to the state's being a physical state or to the state's being a nonphysical state. The state description or introspective report is thus, according to Smart, topic-neutral.

It is perhaps worth noting that to hold that certain mental-state ascriptions are topic-neutral is not thereby to adopt a position of NEUTRAL MONISM. Adopting neutral monism is to take a certain kind of stand on the mind/body problem. Holding that certain ascriptions are topic-neutral is logically independent of any particular stand on the mind/body problem. Indeed, Smart famously advocated the TYPE-IDENTITY THESIS.

transcendental argument, a kind of argument, most closely associated with Immanuel KANT (though, arguably, there are examples that pre-date Kant's) that has (1) as one of its premises an allegedly obvious claim about EXPERIENCE, KNOWLEDGE, or some other feature of one's own mind (e.g., the grasp of certain CONCEPTS or the capacity to entertain some kind of THOUGHT), (2) as another premise a claim about a necessary condition on the truth of the allegedly obvious claim in (1), and (3) a conclusion that the necessary condition in (2) is satisfied. Transcendental arguments often have antiskeptical conclusions (see SKEPTICISM). For example, a transcendental antiskeptical argument famously associated with Kant may be paraphrased as having premises (1) I am aware of my mental states as having an order in time, and (2) it is a necessary condition on my awareness of anything being ordered in time that there be objectively existing entities undergoing alteration. A contemporary antiskeptical argument is due to Hilary PUTNAM and utilizes a version of EXTERNALISM to establish knowledge that he is not a BRAIN IN A VAT. A crucial premise of Putnam's argument is that he could only coherently conceive of the possibility of being a brain in a vat if there really was an external world containing brains and vats (*see also* CAUSAL THEORY OF CONTENT). P. F. Strawson developed a transcendental argument against skepticism about other minds (*see* OTHER MINDS, PROBLEM OF). Employing an early version of the GENERALITY CONSTRAINT, Strawson argued that I can only coherently conceive of myself as being in PAIN if I could likewise conceive of beings other than me being in pain. Not all transcendental arguments target skepticism. For example, Martin Davies has developed a transcendental argument for the existence of a LANGUAGE OF THOUGHT. Not all transcendental arguments postdate Kant. Arguably, the COGITO of DESCARTES can be regarded as a transcendental argument with its premises as follows: (1) I think, and (2) it is a necessary condition on my thinking that I exist.

transcendental ego, in the philosophy of Immanuel KANT, the noumenal self as opposed to the phenomenal self—that is, the self as it is independent of any self that is apparent in EXPERIENCE (*see* APPEARANCE; SELF, THE). Kant held the transcendental ego to be the unknowable self that is responsible for synthesizing experience into a unified whole—the "unity of apperception" or the "I think" that must be capable of accompanying all of our representations (*see* MENTAL REPRESENTATION). Kant also held the transcendental ego to be the source of FREE WILL, the phenomenal self instead being governed by cause and effect.

transcendental idealism, developed by Immanuel KANT as an antidote to both the skeptical EMPIRICISM (*see* SKEPTICISM) held by his British contemporaries and the dogmatic RATIONALISM that dominated philosophy in continental Europe, the view that the truths of mathematics and metaphysics are synthetic and a priori, and are able to have this synthetic a priori status largely in part because space and time are mind-dependent: space being the form of outer EXPERIENCE and time being the form of inner experience. Further, Kant held that empirical knowledge, that is, synthetic a posteriori knowledge of the things that appear to us as located in space and or time, only ever concerns *phenomena* (things as they are given in APPEARANCE) and not *noumena* (things as they are in themselves). *See also* TRANSCENDENTAL ARGUMENT; TRANSCENDENTAL EGO; REALISM; IDEALISM.

transparency (of experience), an alleged property of our conscious experiences (*see* CONSCIOUSNESS; EXPERIENCE) whereby we are incapable of attending to or being conscious of the experiences themselves and can only attend to or be conscious of what the experiences are experiences *of*. According to adherents of this transparency claim, when having, for example, a visual experience of a tree, I cannot become aware of any features of the experience itself but can only be aware of the tree and features of the tree (such as its color and leafiness). Also referred to as the *diaphaneity* of experience, the transparency of experience was first pointed out early in the twentieth century by G. E. Moore and highlighted in the latter part of the century by Gilbert Harman as part of an argument defending FUNCTIONALISM against attacks hinging on QUALIA. Following a line of thought similar to Harman's, defenders of FIRST-ORDER REPRESENTATIONALISM have argued for their position in part by appeal to premises asserting the transparency of experience. It is worth noting that the notion of the transparency of experience is distinct from both of the following other notions philosophers sometimes refer to using "transparency": TRANSPARENCY, REFERENTIAL and TRANSPARENCY (OF THE MIND TO ITSELF).

transparency (of the mind to itself), the view, largely associated with DESCARTES, that if one has some mental state, then one has KNOWLEDGE of that mental state, or at least has a BELIEF to the effect that one has that mental state. *See also* INTROSPECTION; FIRST-PERSON AUTHORITY.

transparency, referential, the ability of co-referring terms to be intersubstitutable without affecting the TRUTH values of the sentences they appear in ("intersubstitutability *salva veritate*"). So, for example, in the sentence "John stood next to Mark Twain," the term "Samuel Clemens," which has the same referent as "Mark Twain," will not, if substituted for "Mark Twain," result in a sentence with a differing truth value. In contrast, a sentence utilizing direct quotation, as in "John said 'I like Mark Twain'" can be true while the sentence generated by substituting a co-referring term for "Mark Twain," such as, "John said 'I like Samuel Clemens'," is false. *See also*, TRUTH; REFERENCE; OPACITY, REFERENTIAL.

trope, a PROPERTY instance. The redness of one apple is a numerically distinct trope from the redness of a numerically distinct apple. The redness of the first apple is distinct from the universal redness. The redness of the first apple is also distinct from the apple itself. The apple itself is a particular red thing, but the trope in question, the redness of that thing, is distinct from the thing itself.

truth, the REPRESENTATION of what *is*, *that* it is and of what is *not*, *that* it is not. Truth is a highly vexed notion over which there is much disagreement among philosophers as to what its ultimate nature consists in. According to some, truth consists in the *correspondence* between representation and reality. For others, truth consists in the *coherence* of a representation with other representations. For yet others, truth may be explicated in terms of *disquotation* and thus there is nothing more said in following a quoted sentence with "is true" than if one simply said the sentence itself. That is, "'Grass is green' is true" conveys no more information than is conveyed by "Grass is green."

Turing machine, conceived of by Alan TURING to explicate a mathematical notion of COMPUTATION—a device consisting of a *finite-state machine* controlling a read/write head, an infinite tape upon which symbols may be written and from which symbols may be read, and a lookup table governing state transitions of the finite-state machine, such as movements up and down the tape and the reading and writing of tape symbols. A *universal Turing machine* is a Turing machine capable of being programmed to emulate any other Turing machine. *See also* ARTIFICIAL INTELLIGENCE.

Turing test, proposed by Alan TURING, a means for detecting genuine implementations of a human-equivalent ARTIFICIAL INTELLIGENCE (AI) whereby an AI passes the test if a human interacting with both the AI and another real human via a text-based interface is unable to tell the difference between the two. Some philosophers have challenged whether these or any behavioral criteria suffice to identify genuine instances of INTELLIGENCE. In connection with this latter issue, see, for example, CHINESE ROOM.

Twin Earth, a planet that is maximally similar to our own planet except for the fact (and whatever is entailed by the fact) that the watery-appearing chemical referred to as "water" by its inhabitants is XYZ, a hypothetical chemical stipulated for purposes of the THOUGHT EXPERIMENT to be chemically distinct from H_2O. The Twin Earth thought experiment serves to probe intuitions (*see* INTUITION) concerning whether and to what degree linguistic and mental CONTENT depends on factors external to a being capable of producing or having such content-bearing states. Thought experiments about Twin Earth figure prominently in discussions concerning EXTERNALISM and INTERNALISM. One example position in such discussions is the externalist position that my intrinsically similar Twin Earth counterpart ("Twin Mandik") and I have beliefs (*see* BELIEF) with different contents when we have the beliefs that each of us would express by asserting "Water is wet." According to this example position, my belief has the WIDE CONTENT that H_2O is wet, whereas Twin Mandik's corresponding belief has the wide content that XYZ is wet. A different example position would be the internalist position that Twin Mandik and I have beliefs with the same NARROW CONTENT—that is, we believe the same thing in having beliefs each of us would express by saying "Water is wet."

type, contrasted with TOKEN, a *universal* or *repeatable* in contrast with a *particular* or *unrepeatable*. For further discussion, see TOKEN.

Type-identity thesis, (*see* PHYSICALISM, REDUCTIVE) a version of PHYSICALISM that is contrasted against the TOKEN-IDENTITY THESIS version of physicalism by affirming that mental types (*see* TYPE) are identical to physical types.

type-token distinction, see the entry on TOKEN for a discussion of the distinction between a TYPE and a token of that type.

type-type identity, *see* PHYSICALISM, REDUCTIVE.

unconscious, the, the sum total of a person's mental states that are not conscious (*see* CONSCIOUSNESS). Alternately, the sum total of a person's mental states that *cannot* be conscious.

underdetermination, perceptual, the failure of the CONTENT of a percept, the content of a state of PERCEPTION, to be determined by a current SENSATION or the current INFORMATION available to the sensory organs. One kind of illustration of perceptual underdetermination involves ambiguous figures such as the DUCK-RABBIT, which may alternately be perceived as a duck or as a rabbit. If, at some particular time, a viewer sees the visual stimulus as a rabbit and not a duck, this perceptual content is not due simply to the information entering the eye at that time, but due instead to results of past EXPERIENCE and co-occurring THOUGHTS and CONCEPTS. Given some other set of co-occurring thoughts and concepts, one and the same visual stimulus may be seen instead as a duck and not a rabbit. Another sort of illustration of perceptual underdetermination was noted by George Berkeley and involves the influence on current perception by past stimulations to sensory organs. One and the same bucket of tepid water may be felt as hot by a hand previously submerged in cold water and felt as cold by a hand previously submerged in hot water.

unity of science, the hypothetical coherence of all the branches of science considered together as a single system. One version of the unity of science hypothesis was due to adherents of LOGICAL POSITIVISM who thought that unification would be achieved via a universal observation language into which all scientific statements could be translated (*see also* PHENOMENALISM). Another version of the unity of science hypothesis is a kind of PHYSICALISM whereby unification would be achieved via the eventual intertheoretical REDUCTION of the so-called special sciences—psychology, biology, and chemistry, to name a few—to physics. One way in which these reductions are envisioned as working is not that each special science would be directly reduced to physics but, instead, psychology would reduce to a branch of biology (likely the biology of nervous systems, *see* NEUROPHILOSOPHY), biology would reduce to chemistry, and chemistry would reduce to physics. Opponents of such a view of the unity of science hold that one or more of the special sciences are autonomous and thus irreducible to physics (*see also* EMERGENCE).

universal, a metaphysical entity alleged to be, in some sense, *present* in multiple distinct particulars—for instance, one and the same PROPERTY of redness is a universal "present" in multiple distinct red things. REALISM about universals holds that universals have either existence or SUBSISTENCE independent of CONCEPTS or predicates. Thus, for example, such a realist may hold that redness is a universal existing independently of anyone's concept of red or the predicative phrase "is red." The position classically opposed to realism about universals is *nominalism*, so-called because early versions of the view held that universals had no existence beyond the names or other parts of language with which we label or describe multiple distinct things. Thus, a nominalist may hold that there's nothing universal present in multiple distinct things beyond the fact that speakers of natural languages such as English apply one and the same word, "red," to multiple distinct things—for example, a pen, an apple, or a flag. *See also* TYPE.

use theory of meaning, due to Ludwig WITTGENSTEIN and Wilfrid SELLARS, the view that the significance of linguistic items is due to their use or role in a language or, as Wittgenstein puts it, in a "language game." Expressed as a slogan, the view is that "meaning is use." Adapted to account for the CONTENT of mental representations (*see* REPRESENTATION, MENTAL), the use theory of meaning becomes the ROLE THEORY OF CONTENT. Due to the uses in question involving multiple relations to other meaningful items, various versions of the use theory of meaning are committed to some form of HOLISM.

vehicle, a REPRESENTATION itself, considered apart from its CONTENT. To illustrate, while the phrase "three letters" has twelve letters, this is a fact about the representational vehicle, not a fact about what is represented. Applied to mental states such as PROPOSITIONAL ATTITUDES, as well as other mental states that have INTENTIONALITY, the notion of a vehicle can be explicated in terms of the mental state itself considered apart from what the mental state is *about*, or, in the case of propositional attitudes, the mental state considered apart from the PROPOSITION toward which it is an attitude. To illustrate, my MEMORY that I had a turkey sandwich for lunch yesterday is an attitude toward a proposition concerning the day before today (or a STATE OF AFFAIRS obtaining the day before today). But the memory itself is a mental state occurring today. The *vehicle* has its existence today, but the *content* concerns an EVENT that occurred yesterday. Another illustration can be given in terms of PERCEPTION: I can perceive that a television screen is bright green and six feet in front of me, but the perception itself is a state of me and makes little sense to be described as being bright green and six feet in front of me. Such a description is a description of the *content* of the perception, not the perception itself.

The content/vehicle distinction may be regarded as analogous to the distinction between use and mention discussed by QUINE and other philosophers. In "'Boston' has six letters," "Boston" is mentioned, not used. In "Boston is a city," "Boston" is used, not mentioned.

verificationism, as an account of CONTENT, the view that the content of a REPRESENTATION is identical with procedures for obtaining experiences (*see* EXPERIENCE) that would make one certain of the representation. Alternately, content is identified with procedures for establishing the TRUTH of a representation. On either construal of what the relevant procedures are, there can be no representation that is meaningful or has content while unverifiable. Alternately, verificationism is an account of *truth* whereby a representation is true if and only if procedures have been (or, alternately, can be) enacted to obtain experiences that make one certain of the representation. On this view, there can be no representation that is true while unverified (or alternately, true while unverifiable).

volition, see WILL, THE.

weakness of will, also known as ᴀᴋʀᴀꜱɪᴀ, the failure to act in accordance with what one judges to be the best action or with what one judges to be the action that one ought to perform. For example, one may have the ʙᴇʟɪᴇꜰ that smoking cigarettes increases chances of getting lung cancer and one may have the ᴅᴇꜱɪʀᴇ to decrease one's chances of getting lung cancer but may nonetheless, due to weakness of will or lack of willpower, have a lapse in resolve and continue to smoke cigarettes. Philosophical problems concerning weakness of will go back at least as far as the ancient Greeks, with Socrates in Plato's dialogue, *Protagoras,* arguing that a person always acts in accordance with what he or she *judges* to be best, and any failure to do what *is* best is due to his or her lack of ᴋɴᴏᴡʟᴇᴅɢᴇ.

what it is like, a phrase often used in philosophy of mind for discussing phenomenal character or ǫᴜᴀʟɪᴀ. Such uses include "*What it is like* to taste a lemon is more like tasting a lime than tasting chocolate" and "A person blind from birth does not know *what it is like* to see red." Perhaps one of the most famous uses of the phrase is due to Thomas Nagel's essay "What Is It Like to Be a Bat?" the titular question of which served to launch Nagel's criticisms of the completeness of physical, objective science. *See* ᴘʜʏꜱɪᴄᴀʟɪꜱᴍ; ᴏʙᴊᴇᴄᴛɪᴠɪᴛʏ; ꜱᴜʙᴊᴇᴄᴛɪᴠɪᴛʏ. A line of thought against physicalism hinging on *what it is like*, similar to Nagel's, was developed by Frank Jackson and others in terms of the now famous ᴋɴᴏᴡʟᴇᴅɢᴇ ᴀʀɢᴜᴍᴇɴᴛ concerning conditions under which one may acquire ᴋɴᴏᴡʟᴇᴅɢᴇ of what it is like to see red. Central to the knowledge argument is a ᴛʜᴏᴜɢʜᴛ ᴇxᴘᴇʀɪᴍᴇɴᴛ concerning Mary, a hypothetical super-neuroscientist who knows all of the objective physical facts about human color vision but has never herself seen red before. Many philosophers share the ɪɴᴛᴜɪᴛɪᴏɴ that Mary does not know what it is like to see red if all she has is knowledge of physical facts and has not herself seen red. The intuition that one could not know what it is like to have certain kinds of ᴇxᴘᴇʀɪᴇɴᴄᴇ (e.g., tasting wine or pineapple) without first undergoing an experience of such a kind was appealed to by John ʟᴏᴄᴋᴇ and David ʜᴜᴍᴇ in their arguments for ᴇᴍᴘɪʀɪᴄɪꜱᴍ. *See also* ᴍᴏʟʏɴᴇᴜx ǫᴜᴇꜱᴛɪᴏɴ; ᴍɪꜱꜱɪɴɢ ꜱʜᴀᴅᴇ ᴏꜰ ʙʟᴜᴇ.

wide content, *see* ᴄᴏɴᴛᴇɴᴛ, ᴡɪᴅᴇ.

will, the, the alleged faculty in virtue of which a person is able to act as he or she wants (*see* ᴀᴄᴛɪᴏɴ). Philosophical debate surrounds the question of whether such a characterization of the will also suffices to characterize FREE WILL, or whether more needs to be said in order to truly describe a will as *free*. Philosophical debate also surrounds the question of whether there is such a thing as WEAKNESS OF WILL. Aside from philosophical debates concerning the problem of free will and the problem of weakness of will, the questions of whether there is such a thing as the will and, if so, what constitutes its nature are philosophical topics in their own right. One kind of approach to these latter sorts of questions is to hold that the will is comprised of special mental states, "willings" or "acts of will," which play a role somewhat akin to the role postulated for SENSE DATA. Whereas sense data play a role at the input interface between the mind and the external world, acts of will play a role at the output interface. Whereas sense data serve as intermediaries of the world's causal effects on the mind, willings serve as intermediaries of the mind's causal effects on the world.

XYZ, the substance called "water" on TWIN EARTH, a crucial THOUGHT EXPERIMENT in discussions of EXTERNALISM and so-called WIDE CONTENT.

zombie, a hypothetical being that is physically, functionally, or behaviorally identical to a normal human but lacks QUALIA or phenomenal CONSCIOUSNESS (*see* CONSCIOUSNESS, PHENOMENAL). The alleged conceivability of zombies has been utilized in arguments put forward by certain dualists (*see* DUALISM, PROPERTY) in versions of the MODAL ARGUMENT. Such a line of argument targets PHYSICALISM in the following way: If physicalism is true, then, at least on many versions of physicalism, it is impossible for beings that are physically identical to be phenomenally distinct. Thus, if it is possible for a being to be physically just like me but to lack qualia, a being we can call "Zombie Mandik," then physicalism is false. Assuming a certain kind of link between CONCEIVABILITY and POSSIBILITY, if Zombie Mandik is conceivable, then Zombie Mandik is possible and physicalism is false. Another way to use an appeal to the possibility of zombies in the philosophy of mind is in developing an argument against FUNCTIONALISM along lines that do not obviously call into question physicalism. According to such an argument, if functionalism is true, then a being who, despite being physically distinct from me, is still functionally equivalent to me, is a being who is also phenomenally like me. So, if a being that has microchips doing what my neurons do for me, a being we can call "Robot Mandik," can possibly lack qualia, then functionalism is false. A similar line of argument, involving not microchips but instead citizens of the nation of China playing the functional roles of neurons, is the CHINESE NATION argument. *See also* CHINESE ROOM.

The Key Thinkers

Aristotle, (384–322 BC) of enormous significance to Western philosophy, second perhaps only to PLATO, Aristotle's influence continues in all areas of philosophy. Most pertinent to the philosophy of mind is Aristotle's reaction against the DUALISM of Plato and the development of an early version of FUNCTIONALISM. Central to Aristotle's rebellion against Plato was Aristotle's rejection of universals (*see* UNIVERSAL) as being Forms having an existence separable from their instances. Aristotle's view, hylomorphism, was that each concrete SUBSTANCE consists in both form and matter. While Aristotle often emphasized form and matter, the form and matter of a thing were just two of the causes or explanatory factors of a thing (*see* EXPLANATION). In addition to the formal cause and material cause of a thing were its final cause (*see* TELEOLOGY) and its efficient cause. To illustrate Aristotle's doctrine of the four causes, consider the explanatory factors that may be invoked in connection with a sword: Its material cause is the metal from which it is made and accounts for its hardness and flexibility; its formal cause is the shape and accounts for its suitability for cutting things; its efficient cause is perhaps most closely associated with what we currently think of as causation and consists of the events that eventuated in the sword's creation; the final cause is the purpose or end to which the sword is put, in this case, serving as a weapon. Most pertinent to the philosophy of mind is Aristotle's doctrine that the soul (*psyche*) is the form of the body. One expression of this view is Aristotle's statement that if the eye were an animal, then sight would be its soul. Aristotle considered the souls of humans as divided into multiple faculties: nutrition, PERCEPTION, and mind (*nous*). While all living things have souls, humans are distinct for having minds. The mind is the faculty of the soul responsible for REASONING, knowing, and understanding. Aristotle construed perception as hylomorphic change: Via mediation of the sensory organs, the perceptible object makes an impression upon the perceiver and the perceiver thereby takes on the form, though not the substance, of the perceived object. Aristotle gives an account of thinking that is analogous to the account of perception. Whereas perception is the reception of perceptible form, thinking is the reception of intelligible form. The contrast between thinking and perception is further marked by the distinction between necessary forms and accidental forms where thinking is the reception of the former and perception the reception of the latter. Aristotle also distinguished between two kinds of intellect: passive intellect and active intellect. Aristotle had suggested, echoing the dualism of Plato, that the active intellect was perhaps separable from the body. See also SENSIBLES, COMMON; WEAKNESS OF WILL.

Representative writings:

De anima

Nicomachean Ethics

Metaphysics

Brentano, Franz, (1838–1917) Brentano's key contributions to the philosophy of mind center on INTENTIONALITY and involve both characterizing what the notion consists in and utilizing the notion to give a general account of mental phenomena. For Brentano, intentionality consists in directedness toward an object and held this to be the case even when the object in question does not exist, as with a unicorn. Regarding mental phenomena in general, Brentano advocated a DUALISM whereby mental phenomena are to be distinguished from physical phenomena by virtue of *only* mental phenomena having intentionality. Brentano also held that *all* mental phenomena have intentionality and sought to define the main categories of mental phenomena in terms of intentionality. Thus did Brentano hold the view that intentionality is the MARK OF THE MENTAL. According to Brentano, there are three main categories of mental phenomena: REPRESENTATION, judgment (which includes BELIEF), and feeling (which includes EMOTION and VOLITION). The three categories may be distinguished in terms of whether and in what manner one takes a stand toward the CONTENT or objects of representation. In judgment, one takes an intellectual stand of either affirming or denying. In feeling, one takes an emotional stand of either loving or hating or, alternately, being either for or against. In representation, no stance is taken and the contents are simply present to one's CONSCIOUSNESS. Further distinguishing features of the three categories concern whether and in what manner mental phenomena may be correct or incorrect (*see* NORMATIVE). Whereas representations are neither correct nor incorrect, judgments and feelings are either correct or incorrect. Further, this correctness or incorrectness is objective (*see* OBJECTIVITY) insofar as what one correctly affirms or loves cannot be correctly denied or hated by another and vice versa.

Brentano denied the existence of abstract entities such as propositions (*see* PROPOSITION) and held that only concrete entities exist. Thus in affirming the existence of a coffee mug, for example, one is not affirming the proposition "A coffee mug exists," one is instead affirming a concrete thing: a coffee mug.

Representative writing:

Psychology from an Empirical Standpoint (1874)

Chalmers, David, (1966–) known primarily for his work on CONSCIOUSNESS (especially QUALIA) highlighting the significance of the HARD PROBLEM, advancing various lines of thought against PHYSICALISM (especially through versions of the MODAL ARGUMENT, the KNOWLEDGE ARGUMENT, and the EXPLANATORY-GAP ARGUMENT), and developing a version of property dualism (*see* DUALISM, PROPERTY) alleged to be consistent with both NATURALISM and strong AI (*see* ARTIFICIAL INTELLIGENCE).

Representative writing:

The Conscious Mind (1996)

Chisholm, Roderick, (1916–1999) Chisholm followed BRENTANO in holding that INTENTIONALITY was the MARK OF THE MENTAL. Central to his views in EPISTEMOLOGY was his advocacy of foundationalism and his view that there existed certain incorrigible states of mind (*see* INCORRIGIBILITY). In his work on PERSONAL IDENTITY and the nature of the self (*see* SELF, THE), he rejected both HUME's bundle view of the self and KANT's view that there is an unknowable, noumenal self. Among Chisholm's views on the self, especially notable are those relating to ACTION and FREE WILL. He revived a distinction from medieval philosophy between "immanent" causation (causation by agents [*see* AGENT]) and "transeunt" causation (causation by events [*see* EVENT]). He held the self to be the cause, in the "immanent" sense of "cause," of its own actions.

Representative writings:

Perceiving (1957)

Theory of Knowledge (1966)

Person and Object (1976)

The First Person (1981)

Chomsky, Noam, (1928–) Chomsky's significance for the philosophy of mind is due chiefly to his work as a linguist on questions concerning the acquisition and nature of KNOWLEDGE of language. Regarding the acquisition of knowledge of language, as Chomsky sets forth in his POVERTY OF THE STIMULUS argument, a child's grasp of a language exceeds what can be learned from the small samples that arise in the company of parents and peers. Chomsky rejects proposals that language acquisition is along the lines consistent with

EMPIRICISM and BEHAVIORISM and embraces instead a kind of NATIVISM. With regard to the nature of knowledge of language, it consists of an innate initial state, which Chomsky refers to as a Universal Grammar that embodies universal principles of linguistic competence and a set of parameters that are adjusted as the child moves from the initial state to a state that constitutes knowledge of, for instance, English or Hungarian. One of the key aspects of the Universal Grammar is that it is *generative* and thus allows for the production and comprehension of a potentially infinite set of sentences (*see also* PRODUCTIVITY).

Representative writings:

Syntactic Structures (1957)

Aspects of the Theory of Syntax (1965)

Language and Mind (1972)

Rules and Representations (1980)

Churchland, Patricia (1943–) most notable for founding and advocating the development of NEUROPHILOSOPHY, Churchland produced a body of work on understanding the mind from the point of view of a kind of NATURALISM that is deeply skeptical of both the SYMBOLICISM dominant in many areas of COGNITIVE SCIENCE and the a priori methods (such as CONCEPTUAL ANALYSIS) dominant in many areas of traditional contemporary philosophy. Often in collaboration with husband Paul CHURCHLAND, Patricia Churchland advocates interdisciplinary approaches to understanding the mind/brain that involve philosophical arguments that are highly deferential to the cognitive neurosciences.

Representative writings:

Neurophilosophy (1986)

Brain-wise (2002)

Churchland, Paul (1942–) a student of Wilfrid SELLARS, Churchland was heavily influenced by his teacher's SCIENTIFIC REALISM and view of the status of FOLK PSYCHOLOGY as a theory comparable to scientific theories. Churchland was skeptical, however, of the worth of folk psychology as the basis for a scientific understanding of the mind/brain and developed a widely discussed version of

ELIMINATIVE MATERIALISM. Churchland, often in collaboration with wife Patricia CHURCHLAND, developed a body of philosophical work highly influenced by the neurosciences and CONNECTIONISM (*see also* NEUROPHILOSOPHY). Churchland argued, in opposition to EPIPHENOMENALISM, DUALISM, and the KNOWLEDGE ARGUMENT, that brain states could, with sufficient neuroscientific training, be introspected (*see* INTROSPECTION) as brain states. Churchland thus opposed the claim that it is an obvious point of PHENOMENOLOGY that each of us, in enjoying states of CONSCIOUSNESS, is in direct contact with nonphysical QUALIA. Part of Churchland's case for the possibility of training introspection to be sensitive to neurophysiology was grounded in his opposition to the MODULARITY of perceptual systems (*see* PERCEPTION). Churchland held, in opposition to Jerry FODOR, that perception is cognitively penetrable and thus the way in which things are perceived is influenced by the CONCEPTS acquired and deployed by the perceiver.

Representative writings:

Scientific Realism and the Plasticity of Mind (1979)

Matter and Consciousness (1984)

A Neurocomputational Perspective (1989)

The Engine of Reason, the Seat of the Soul (1995)

Neurophilosophy at Work (2007)

Davidson, Donald (1917–2003) Davidson's highly influential work on actions and events (*see* ACTION; EVENT) gave rise to his widely discussed thesis of ANOMALOUS MONISM and related ideas such as SUPERVENIENCE and SWAMP MAN. He defended an extreme form of HOLISM concerning the attribution of PROPOSITIONAL ATTITUDES. He held REASONS to be causes, but this view had several problematic features to it. According to Davidson's anomalous monism, mental events are not subsumed under laws when mental descriptions of the events are used but are subsumed under laws only when physical descriptions are used. So, while a reason may be token-identical to a physical event (*see* TOKEN-IDENTITY THESIS) it is not *as* a reason that it is governed by natural laws concerning causes and effects. It thus seems that it is not *as* a reason that it counts as a cause.

Representative writings:

Essays on Actions and Events (1980)

Essays on Truth and Interpretation (1984)

Dennett, Daniel (1942–) Dennett's highly influential and widely discussed work in philosophy of mind focuses primarily on the three problems of INTENTIONALITY, CONSCIOUSNESS, and FREE WILL. A defender of PHYSICALISM, FUNCTIONALISM, and ARTIFICIAL INTELLIGENCE, Dennett's work is distinctive in the emphasis it puts on NATURALISM and the applicability of the natural sciences to philosophy. Dennett is especially interested in developing links between the Darwinian theory of evolution by natural selection and problems in the philosophy of mind and COGNITIVE SCIENCE (*see also* TELEOLOGY). Highly influenced by RYLE, WITTGENSTEIN, and QUINE, Dennett is highly skeptical about overly realistic (*see* REALISM) approaches to understanding the nature of intentionality and argues instead that intentionality is best understood via what Dennett has dubbed the INTENTIONAL STANCE. For similar reasons and under similar influences, Dennett has also mounted sharp attacks against the notion of QUALIA and has developed his own physicalistic theory of consciousness, the MULTIPLE-DRAFTS THEORY OF CONSCIOUSNESS.

Representative writings:

Elbow Room (1984)

The Intentional Stance (1987)

Consciousness Explained (1991)

Darwin's Dangerous Idea (1995)

Descartes, René, (1591–1650) There is little doubt that Descartes is the most significant figure in the philosophy of mind. He looms large not just in philosophy of mind; he is a towering figure in philosophy in general as well as in mathematics and the natural sciences. Many of the basic concepts of analytic geometry are due to Descartes, including the Cartesian coordinate system, which is named after him. His contributions to other areas of philosophy, especially in EPISTEMOLOGY and the problem of SKEPTICISM about the external world, have been enormously influential. But what's been of central significance to the development of the philosophy of mind has been Descartes's influence on the subsequent thinking about the MIND/BODY PROBLEM via his arguments for substance dualism (*see* DUALISM, SUBSTANCE). Also influential for the philosophy of mind was Descartes's defenses of RATIONALISM and attacks on EMPIRICISM. One line of thought aimed at demonstrating that KNOWLEDGE is not wholly dependent on sensory PERCEPTION is Descartes's famous COGITO. Another is Descartes's discussion of the wax in his *Meditations*: A piece of wax that starts as a solid then melts while next to a fire is known to persist as one and the same thing despite changing all of its sensible properties (odor, color, etc.) (*see also* SECONDARY QUALITIES). Descartes concluded that the knowledge thereby gained was not due solely to the senses.

Representative writings:

Rules for the Direction of the Mind (1628)

Discourse on Method (1637)

Meditations on First Philosophy (1641)

Principles of Philosophy (1644)

The Passions of the Soul (1649)

Dretske, Fred (1932–) Dretske's earlier work largely concerned issues in EPISTEMOLOGY and later shifted more toward concerns in the philosophy of mind, especially MENTAL CAUSATION, INTENTIONALITY, and CONSCIOUSNESS. Dretske introduced and defended a distinction between epistemic seeing and nonepistemic seeing (*see* SEEING). He developed an account of INFORMATION and applied it in an account of KNOWLEDGE. Regarding mental causation and the theory of ACTION, Dretske developed a view that behavior is not bodily movement caused by REASONS but the *causing* of bodily movement by reasons. He is a major proponent of applications of TELEOLOGY to the problem of intentionality (*see also* TELEOSEMANTICS). His resultant view is a version of EXTERNALISM. In his most recent work, he applies his account of intentionality to understanding QUALIA and CONSCIOUSNESS. He defends a version of FIRST-ORDER REPRESENTATIONALISM about conscious EXPERIENCE. According to Dretske, experiential CONTENT is determined by evolutionary history, whereas THOUGHT content is determined by learning history.

Representative writings:

Seeing and Knowing (1969)

Knowledge and the Flow of Information (1981)

Explaining Behavior (1988)

Naturalizing the Mind (1995)

Fodor, Jerry (1935–) Widely influential in philosophy of mind and COGNITIVE SCIENCE, Fodor is well known for his defenses of the representational theory of mind, especially as articulated in the form of the LANGUAGE OF THOUGHT hypothesis (*see also* SYMBOLICISM). He is also well known for defenses of the MODULARITY of the mind and the autonomy of psychology from neuroscience due to considerations of MULTIPLE REALIZABILITY, as well as for attacks on HOLISM and CONNECTIONISM.

Representative writings:

The Language of Thought (1975)

The Modularity of Mind (1983)

Psychosemantics (1987)

Holism: a Shopper's Guide (1992, with Ernest Lepore)

The Elm and the Expert (1995)

Hume, David (1711–1777) Of enormous importance to the development of western philosophy, much of Hume's contributions are consequences he drew from the motto of EMPIRICISM that there is nothing in the mind that is not first in the senses. Many of Hume's conclusions were forms of SKEPTICISM about topics such as causation, the self (*see* SELF, THE), and God.

To illustrate how empiricism can drive such a skepticism, consider a Humean treatment of causation. If we really do have an adequate conception of causation, then we should be able to distinguish, in sensory EXPERIENCE, the difference between one event's *causing* another event and one event's preceding another *coincidentally*. However, there being no apparent distinction between causation and mere coincidental correlation given to experience, it seems that we don't really have any basis for saying that one event causes another. The kind of skepticism here promoted can be quite radical. It goes beyond questioning whether we can ever *know* that such-and-such is the case (*see* KNOWLEDGE) and questions whether we can even have a *coherent idea* or conception of such-and-such (*see* CONCEPTS). It should be noted, however, that Hume likely did not follow such skepticism to its radical extreme. Hume did not so much deny that we had an idea of causation as suggest that our idea of causation arises naturally in us as a reaction to a series of repeated conjunctions of events, such as the repeated observation that the release of an object is followed by the falling of that object.

Despite avoiding the absolute extreme of skepticism, a strand of thought along relatively radical empirical/skeptical lines colors much of Hume's philosophy, especially those portions most directly relevant to the philosophy of mind. Hume held the main elements of the mind to be perceptions (*see* PERCEPTION), which were divided into sensory impressions (*see also* SENSATION) and ideas, which are copies of impressions. Hume sometimes characterized ideas as being less vivid than impressions, though the main difference between ideas and impressions is that impressions are the causal antecedents of ideas. The processes of thought are largely characterized in terms of the association of ideas. One thing that Hume's perception-based ONTOLOGY of the mind left no room for was any view of the self as an independent SUBSTANCE. Hume wrote that when we attempt to have a perception of ourselves, all that we are greeted with is "a bundle or collection of different perceptions, which succeed each other with an inconceivable rapidity, and are in a perpetual flux and movement."

On the topic of FREE WILL, Hume defended a version of compatibilism. He held that there were no uncaused actions. Any such "actions" would not be evaluable as moral or immoral. Actions that arise freely are those that are caused by us and unimpeded by any outside factor.

See also MISSING SHADE OF BLUE.

Representative writings:

A Treatise of Human Nature, Book I (1739), Book II (1740)

An Abstract of a Treatise of Human Nature (1740)

An Enquiry Concerning Human Understanding (1748)

An Enquiry Concerning the Principles of Morals (1751)

Kant, Immanuel (1724–1804) A towering figure in the history of Western philosophy, comparable in significance to PLATO and ARISTOTLE, with wide-ranging influences on subsequent developments in metaphysics, epistemology, and ethics. Central to Kant's philosophy is his TRANSCENDENTAL IDEALISM and his employment of his transcendental method (*see* TRANSCENDENTAL ARGUMENT), which involves drawing inferences concerning the conditions necessary for the possibility of certain forms of KNOWLEDGE or EXPERIENCE. Kant held empirical knowledge to involve knowledge of appearances, which always involved things appearing in time and sometimes in space as well. Empirical judgment involves the subsuming of sensory inputs, intuitions (*see* INTUITION), under CONCEPTS. Time and space were themselves contributions of the mind, though they are not themselves either concepts or intuitions. Time and space instead constitute the *form* of inner and outer sense, with time being the form of inner sense and space being the form of outer sense. The mental constituency of time and space was supposed by Kant to account for the applicability of mathematics, geometry, and other "synthetic a priori" truths to empirical reality. Contrasted with things as they appear, phenomenal things, was a realm of things in themselves, noumenal things. The phenomenal/noumenal distinction applied also to the self (*see* SELF, THE). The noumenal self, the TRANSCENDENTAL EGO, accounted for, among other things, the freedom of the will (*see* FREE WILL; WILL, THE): freedom is the causality of the noumenal self.

Representative writings:

Critique of Pure Reason (1781)

Prolegomena to Any Future Metaphysics That Will Be Able to Present Itself as a Science (1783)

Groundwork of the Metaphysics of Morals (1785)

Critique of Practical Reason (1788)

Critique of Judgment (1790)

Kim, Jaegwon (1934–) Kim's earlier work focused on the notion of an EVENT, and later work focused on SUPERVENIENCE and MENTAL CAUSATION. Kim defended an account of an event as the INSTANTIATION of a PROPERTY at a time. Such a view of events is comparatively more "fine-grained" than the competing accounts of events defended by philosophers such as Donald DAVIDSON and W.V.O. QUINE. On Kim's view, a person's chewing gum and walking at noon resolves into at least two events: that person's chewing gum at noon and that person's walking at noon. On more "coarse-grained" accounts of events. For instance, where an event is the set of temporal parts of a physical object, there may only be one event picked out by the description of a person as "walking and chewing gum at noon."

Much of Kim's work developing the implications for philosophy of mind of the notion of supervenience has served to put pressure on the tenability of nonreductive physicalism (see PHYSICALISM, NONREDUCTIVE; PHYSICALISM, REDUCTIVE). Related, and central to his work on mental causation, is his development of his EXPLANATORY EXCLUSION argument. Kim has expressed the worry that unless the supervenience of the mental on the physical is explained by the mental reducing to the physical, then an EPIPHENOMENALISM about the mental must follow.

Representative writings:

"Causation, nomic subsumption, and the concepts of event" (1973)

"The myth of nonreductive materialism" (1989)

"Supervenience as a philosophical concept" (1990)

Supervenience and Mind (1993)

Mind in a Physical World (1998)

Physicalism, or Something Near Enough (2005)

Kripke, Saul (1940–) Kripke's work in the philosophy of language and logic led to contributions in the philosophy of mind such as an early and influential version of the MODAL ARGUMENT against PHYSICALISM and groundwork that influenced the subsequent development (by other philosophers such as Hilary PUTNAM) of the CAUSAL THEORY OF CONTENT and EXTERNALISM. Kripke also produced a controversial interpretation of the PRIVATE-LANGUAGE ARGUMENT of Ludwig WITTGENSTEIN. Due to the controversial nature of Kripke's interpretation of Wittgenstein, philosophers often refer to the version of Wittgenstein there presented as "Kripkenstein."

Representative writings:

Naming and Necessity (1980)

Wittgenstein on Rules and Private Language (1982)

Lewis, David (1941–2001) Lewis's contributions to the philosophy of mind involved the development of various physicalistic theses and defenses of PHYSICALISM. The brand of physicalism that Lewis favored was a kind of FUNCTION-ALISM whereby functional analyses where obtained by collecting the mass of commonsense platitudes about mental states—platitudes such as "People who desire something tend to seek it out," "People who believe that something will cause painful experiences will fear it," and so on—and then codifying such mental states in the form of theories expressed as sets of Ramsey sentences (see RAMSEY SENTENCE. See also RAMSIFICATION). Lewis saw the resultant functionalism as compatible with the TYPE-IDENTITY THESIS (see also TYPE-TYPE IDENTITY). The functional roles described by the Ramsified theory, discovered by consulting commonsense platitudes, were open to be identified with entities discoverable in the physical sciences, including neuroscience.

Lewis was an influential defender of the *ability hypothesis*, a physicalist response to the KNOWLEDGE ARGUMENT whereby it is objected that KNOWLEDGE of WHAT IT IS LIKE to see red is not, as presupposed by the knowledge argument, a kind of PROPOSITIONAL KNOWLEDGE, but instead, a kind of KNOW-HOW. Defenders of the ability hypothesis hold that the knowledge of what it is like to see red is constituted by an ability to recognize and imagine red things (see also IMAGERY; MEMORY).

Representative writings:

"An argument for the identity theory" (1966)

"Psychophysical and theoretical identifications" (1970)

"Mad pain and Martian pain" (1980)

"What experience teaches" (1990)

Locke, John, (1632–1704), An influential defender of modern EMPIRICISM and opponent of RATIONALISM, Locke rejected especially the rationalist thesis that there exist any innate ideas (see INNATENESS). Locke held that the a person's mind enters life as a "*tabula rasa,*" a blank slate upon which *ideas* are written via the receipt of sensations (see SENSATION) through the organs of sensory EXPERIENCE. The receipt of sensations also provides raw material to the processes of reflection or SELF-CONSCIOUSNESS, held by Locke to be "that notice which the mind takes of its own operations and the manner of them."

Locke divided ideas into simple ideas and complex ideas. Simple ideas are sensory ideas such as redness, hotness, and sweetness. Complex ideas are built up out of other ideas (out of other complex ideas as well as out of simple ideas). Whereas we cannot create simple ideas, we can create complex ideas, as in the case of the ideas of mythical and fictional entities.

An additional feature of simple ideas, according to Locke, is that it is possible that they have different causes than we ordinarily take them to have. He expressed this thesis in what seems to be the earliest recorded version of the INVERTED SPECTRUM hypothesis.

Two crucial features of Locke's account of ideas are that they are the objects of which the mind is most directly aware and that they are representations (*see* MENTAL REPRESENTATION) allowing the mind to be aware, albeit indirectly, of the world external to it. These features of Locke's account of ideas figured prominently both in his account of sensory perception and in his account of linguistic communication. Locke's account of sensory perception was a version of REPRESENTATIVE REALISM, whereby perception of material objects is indirect and mediated by ideas, of which we are directly aware and which are caused by material objects. Among the external-world items that we have indirect awareness of are the various items in spoken and written language. The meaning that such signs express is, according to Locke, the private ideas that, in the mind of the speaker or author, are the causal source of the communicative items.

One of the earliest versions of modern theories of PERSONAL IDENTITY is due to Locke, who held that a person's identity over time is due to neither a material nor immaterial SUBSTANCE but to a continuity in consciousness due to continuities in MEMORY.

Locke articulated a well-known distinction between PRIMARY QUALITIES and SECONDARY QUALITIES.

Representative writing:

An Essay Concerning Human Understanding (1690)

Millikan, Ruth (1933–) One of the most widely known defenders of TELEO-SEMANTICS, an approach to understanding the INTENTIONALITY of language and THOUGHT by reference to a teleological notion of function (*see* FUNCTION, TELEOLO-GICAL) grounded in the Darwinian theory of evolution by natural selection.

Representative writings:

Language, Thought, and Other Biological Categories (1984)

White Queen Psychology and Other Essays for Alice (1993)

On Clear and Confused Ideas (2000)

The Varieties of Meaning: The 2002 Jean Nicod Lectures (2004)

Language: A Biological Model (2005)

Plato (427–347 BC) There is little doubt that Plato is the single most significant figure in Western philosophy. Plato's philosophy comes to us in the form of many dialogues in which the central recurring participant and main biographic subject is the philosopher Socrates (469–399 BC). Though others besides Plato wrote of Socrates, Socrates left no writings of his own. Plato's influence is enormous and wide ranging and no less so in the philosophy of mind.

Central to Plato's contributions to the philosophy of mind are his theory of the Forms and the account of the soul as a knower of the Forms. Plato's Forms are also known as *ideas*, though the contemporary reader should take care to note that the Forms are not supposed to be mental entities or products of the mind. They are instead objective, unchanging universals grasped through the intellect (*see* UNIVERSAL; PROPERTY). The changing entities available to the senses are but imperfect imitations of the unchanging, eternal Forms.

Plato held knowledge, at least at its highest levels, to be the grasp of universal truths via intellectual contact with the Forms. Such knowledge was not acquired in a person's lifetime, but acquired by his or her immaterial soul before birth. (This is Plato's doctrine of *anamnesis*.) Certain techniques, such as the Socratic method of asking a student certain questions (what we still refer to today as "teaching by the Socratic method"), could aid a student to come to remember the knowledge that the trauma of birth made him or her temporarily forget.

In Plato's extremely famous dialogue the *Republic*, he outlines an account of the soul through an extended analogy concerning the various portions of a well-governed state. The soul of a just person consists of three integrated and cooperating parts: a part that reasons and understands, a part that is assertive and is capable of anger and competitiveness, and a part that consists of such appetites as those for food and sex. The just person is governed by the REASONING part, but an educated intellect is insufficient for a well-functioning soul: The emotional and appetitive parts themselves must be trained so that they do not overpower the intellect, but nonetheless provide sufficient force to motivate it.

As the just person is ruled by a part that attains understanding, the just state must be governed by a *philosopher king*. Plato describes the education of a philosopher king as beginning with the imperfect knowledge gained through the senses and culminating in a perfected knowledge of the Forms.

The stages of this ascent to the highest level of knowledge are given in the analogy of the *divided line*. The divided line may be envisioned as a vertical line divided into four segments. The bottom two segments correspond to the sensible world and the top two segments correspond to the intelligible world. The bottommost of the four corresponds to mere "shadows and reflections." The next from the bottom corresponds to natural and manufactured material objects. The third segment concerns truths derived by intellectual contemplation of the material objects. The topmost segment involves knowledge of universal truths that do not depend on the entities of the lower segments.

In the famous *allegory of the cave*, Plato likens the ascent to this highest level of knowledge to a slave who finally escapes from a life wherein he was chained from birth inside a cave and forced to look at only shadows of puppets cast upon the cave wall. When escaping the cave to see the real world in the light of the sun, the slave is initially blinded and dazzled and takes this outer world to be a departure from reality. But in time, the freed slave comes to see the illuminated outer world as genuine reality, a reality that he is now free to comprehend. By analogy, the world of Forms initially illuminated by the light of reason may dazzle and blind us and make us yearn for an earlier, though less perfect, realm of familiar, though false, entities.

Plato's views of the soul and of knowledge serve as highly influential precursors to subsequent forms of DUALISM and RATIONALISM.

Representative writings:

Meno

Phaedo

Republic

Putnam, Hilary (1926–) Early defender and eventual critic of FUNCTIONALISM and developer of an influential version of EXTERNALISM.

Early defender of functionalism. Putnam developed, in the 1950s and 1960s, an early version of FUNCTIONALISM. Distinctive of Putnam's functionalism were two chief components, both of which strongly influenced subsequent discussions of functionalism. The first component consisted in an opposition to the identification of mental types (*see* TYPE), with neurophysiological types similar to those embraced by defenders of the TYPE-IDENTITY THESIS. Putnam instead promoted the MULTIPLE REALIZABILITY of mental types by physical (chemical, biological) types (*see also* REALIZATION). The second chief component of Putnam's functionalism was the suggestion that mental states be identified with states of COMPUTATION. While it is common to associate this sort of view with the suggestion that a human mind is equivalent to a TURING MACHINE, a more accurate description of Putnam's specific proposal is that a human be regarded as a *probabilistic automaton*. Regardless of these precise details, the suggestion that THOUGHT and REASONING be construed as the sorts of things achievable by a mechanical computing device was of central importance to ARTIFICIAL INTELLIGENCE and COGNITIVE SCIENCE.

Meanings just ain't in the head. In the 1970s, Putnam developed an account of the relation of linguistic meaning to mental states that was widely influential on subsequent discussions of EXTERNALISM. Putnam developed the famous THOUGHT EXPERIMENT concerning TWIN EARTH wherein what looks like water and is called "water" by its inhabitants is chemically distinct from H_2O (*see* XYZ). Putnam urged that despite any psychological/functional similarities between the inhabitants of Earth and the inhabitants of Twin Earth, Earthlings and Twin Earthlings meant different things by their "water" utterances. As Putnam summarized his central conclusion, "Meanings just ain't in the head."

Eventual critic of functionalism. In the 1980s, Putnam came to abandon the functionalism that he had earlier helped pioneer. One of the key features of the mind is INTENTIONALITY, and Putnam came to be skeptical of functionalism's ability to account for intentionality. The problem can be seen if we interpret functionalism as defining mental states solely in terms of computational functions concerning relations that obtain entirely within a system such as a brain. Putnam's earlier work on how "meanings just ain't in the head" led him to think that an account of intentionality couldn't be restricted to computational processes definable in terms of what goes on solely in the head.

Representative writings

"Minds and machines" (1960)

"The meaning of meaning" (1975)

Reason, Truth, and History (1981)

Representation and Reality (1988)

Quine, Willard van Orman, (1908–2000) A towering figure in twentieth-century philosophy, Quine's influence on the philosophy of mind grows out of his critiques of EMPIRICISM, his tendency toward BEHAVIORISM, his commitment to NATURALISM, and his hostility toward INTENSIONALITY.

Against the analytic/synthetic distinction. In his famous paper "Two dogmas of empiricism" the two dogmas under attack are the analytic/synthetic distinction and a form of REDUCTIONISM known as PHENOMENALISM. The alleged distinction between the analytic and the synthetic is a distinction between (analytic) sentences such as "All bachelors are unmarried," which are true in virtue of their meaning and (synthetic) sentences such as "Some bachelors are brunette," which, if true, cannot be deduced from meaning alone and are knowable only through EXPERIENCE. Quine questioned whether there were such things as analytic truths by arguing that the very notion was either definable in an intolerably circular way (invoking notions of meaning that themselves presupposed a notion of analyticity) or based on a supposition of unreviasability that Quine questioned.

Hostility toward phenomenalism and sense data. Quine was hostile to the empiricist proposal of phenomenalism whereby it is alleged that the meaning of a statement is reducible to the experiences that would verify it. Quine's objection to phenomenalism depended on his allegiance to a form of HOLISM. Quine held that sentences did not "face the tribunal of experience" one at a time but as groups of interconnected sentences. And for any experience that seemed to contradict a sentence, the sentence itself could be held on to by simply rejecting some other sentence in the interanimating web of sentences.

Quine's objections to sense data (and related points can apply to QUALIA) is that he thought they were poor replacements for physical objects and that there were no compelling reasons for positing them in addition to physical objects.

Quine's flight from intension. Quine argued that an analysis of the kind of logic and language sufficient for the purposes of science and mathematics revealed that intensionality, in its various guises (*see* POSSIBILITY; PROPOSITIONAL ATTITUDE) is dispensable.

Indeterminacy of translation and inscrutability of reference. Through his famous arguments concerning "gavagai" and the project of RADICAL TRANSLATION, Quine came to be convinced of the theses of the INDETERMINACY OF TRANSLATION and the INSCRUTABILITY OF REFERENCE. The development of these theses in Quine's thought led him to a general hostility toward any suggestion that there could be determinate facts of the matter about meaning and reference. Such views relate as well to a skepticism about INTENTIONALITY and thus fit well with various worries Quine raised about propositional attitudes.

No distinction between reduction and elimination. Quine's thesis that there are no determinate facts concerning what a word refers to has important implications for debates within PHYSICALISM between advocates of ELIMINATIVE MATERIALISM and reductionism (*see* PHYSICALISM, REDUCTIVE). This debate may be portrayed as taking place between two philosophers over whether a word such as "pain" or "belief" should be eliminated from our vocabulary in favor of descriptions in a neuroscientific vocabulary (eliminative materialism) or instead retained but defined in terms of neuroscientific vocabulary. However, that there could be a substantial debate between these two positions pre-supposes that there is some determinate fact of the matter about what "pain" or "belief" really mean or really refer to.

Naturalized epistemology. One aspect of Quine's philosophy that perhaps had the most direct effects on the philosophy of mind was his advocacy of a kind of naturalism expressed as the view that philosophy is continuous with the natural sciences and that philosophy has no privileged method or point of view from which to criticize scientific claims. Investigations of the mind and knowledge cannot do better than use scientific methods, and the closest thing to traditionally conceived philosophy that is worth doing is when science turns its attention to itself.

Representative writings:

From a Logical Point of View: 9 Logico-Philosophical Essays (1953)

Word and Object (1960)

Ontological Relativity and Other Essays (1969)

Rosenthal, David (1939–) most well known for his development of his HIGHER-ORDER-THOUGHT THEORY OF CONSCIOUSNESS, built on the idea that a conscious mental state is a mental state of which one is conscious (see also SELF-CONSCIOUSNESS). Rosenthal also developed an account of sensory qualities—his "homomorphism theory," so called for the structural resemblance posited between the similarities and differences between properties of perceptible objects in the external world on the one hand and, on the other hand, the similarities and differences between the mental qualities causally occasioned during instances of perceiving an object.

Representative writing:

Consciousness and Mind (2005)

Ryle, Gilbert (1900–1982) Ryle's general approach to philosophy was to employ careful analyses of language to deflate what he saw as the over-inflated claims and recurrent mistakes made by other philosophers. Of special note, especially as pertains to philosophy of mind, was the result of Ryle's turning his attention to the mind as conceived of in the substance DUALISM of René DESCARTES (see also DUALISM). The result was Ryle's enormously influential book, THE CONCEPT OF MIND. See also GHOST IN THE MACHINE; CATEGORY MISTAKE; BEHAVIORISM.

Representative writings:

The Concept of Mind (1949)

Dilemmas (1954)

Searle, John (1932–) Perhaps best known for his critiques of both the research program of ARTIFICIAL INTELLIGENCE and the versions of FUNCTIONALISM that seek to explain cognition in terms of COMPUTATION (*see also* COGNITIVE SCIENCE). The most famous of these critiques is one based on Searle's thought experiment of the CHINESE ROOM, the gist of which is that since it is possible in principle for Searle to follow a "Chinese understanding" program without himself understanding Chinese, understanding (and other aspects of cognition) cannot be reduced to the following of a program. Another of Searle's lines of thought against computational explanations of cognition is based on his claim that whether something counts as performing computation is an observer-relative phenomenon whereas whether a person is capable of cognition does not depend on that person being observed by anyone. Related to this line of thought is a distinction that Searle draws between original and derived INTENTIONALITY. Examples of derived intentionality include written words that depend on an interpretation for their meaning. The interpretations, however, are themselves constituted by the thoughts of interpreters (*see* THOUGHT). How do these thoughts themselves acquire their intentionality? Searle's answer is that however the intentionality of mental states arises, it is not derived via interpretation. Thus are thoughts instances of original intentionality. Another classification of aspects of intentionality due to Searle is his development of the notion of DIRECTION OF FIT.

Another notable thesis of Searle's is his *connection principle*, according to which all mental states are such that it is possible in principle for them to be conscious (*see* CONSCIOUSNESS, STATE).

Representative writings:

Intentionality: An Essay in the Philosophy of Mind (1983)

Minds, Brains, and Science: The 1984 Reith Lectures (1984)

The Rediscovery of the Mind (1992)

Sellars, Wilfrid (1912–1989) Sellars is perhaps best known for his critique of the notion, central to various versions of EMPIRICISM, of the GIVEN in EXPERIENCE. He regarded this notion as "the myth of the given" (*see* GIVEN, MYTH OF THE). Sellars was also an early developer of FUNCTIONALISM, a critic of PRIVILEDGED ACCESS and other kinds of FIRST-PERSON AUTHORITY, and a pioneer in the development of the influential idea that FOLK PSYCHOLOGY should be regarded as a theory on par with scientific theories (*see* SCIENTIFIC REALISM). According to this last view, the central entities of folk psychology, such as beliefs and impressions (*see* BELIEF; IMPRESSION), are theoretical posits just as much as electrons and electromagnetic waves are posits. (One notable philosopher of mind influenced by the theoretical status of folk psychology is Sellars's student, Paul CHURCHLAND, who employed the idea in his development of ELIMINATIVE MATERIALISM.)

Representative writings:

"EMPIRICISM AND THE PHILOSOPHY OF MIND" (1956)

Science, Perception and Reality (1963)

Science and Metaphysics: Variations on Kantian Themes (1968)

Wittgenstein, Ludwig (1889–1951) agreed by many to be the greatest philosopher of the twentieth century. His philosophical prose is highly idiosyncratic, consisting of collections of aphorisms, jokes, and snippets of conversation with himself. His work is largely regarded as falling into an early period and a late period, with the respective representative writings of the two periods being his *Tractatus Logico-Philosophicus* and *Philosophical Investigations*. The *Tractatus* was concerned with sketching the limits of logic, language, and the world itself. One of the theses expressed in this work is that the self (*see* SELF, THE) is not to be found *in* the world but is instead a *limit of* the world. In the *Tractatus*, Wittgenstein advanced the view that the world is a totality of facts, each of which is *pictured* by a proposition. This is a version of the RESEMBLANCE THEORY OF CONTENT. In his later work, Wittgenstein abandons such an account of content or meaning to embrace instead the view that *meaning is use* (*see* USE THEORY OF MEANING). Part of what such a view is supposed to entail is that there is a wide heterogeneity of what meanings can consist in, since there is a wide heterogeneity uses to which words are put. Not only are different words and expressions put to different uses, but an individual word, such as the word "game," can have a wide variety of dissimilar uses related not by a uniform set of common properties but instead related by FAMILY RESEMBLANCE. Other key features of Wittgenstein's later work involved his attacks on the idea of mental states as essentially private (*see* PRIVLEGED ACCESS), especially as developed in his PRIVATE-LANGUAGE ARGUMENT.

Representative writings:

Tractatus Logico-Philosophicus (1921)

Philosophical Investigations (1953)

The Key Texts

Chalmers, David. *The Conscious Mind* **(1996).** Focusing on the aspects of CONSCIOUSNESS having to do with QUALIA and WHAT IT IS LIKE (*see* CONSCIOUSNESS, PHENOMENAL), Chalmers develops attacks on PHYSICALISM and arguments for his positive view, *Naturalistic Dualism*, a kind of property dualism (*see* DUALISM, PROPERTY). Chalmers emphasizes the centrality of the so-called HARD PROBLEM of explaining consciousness (*see* EXPLANATION). One of his key attacks on physicalism is a version of the EXPLANATORY GAP argument. Another is a version of the MODAL ARGUMENT that hinges on the CONCEIVABILITY and POSSIBILITY of a ZOMBIE—a being that is behaviorally, functionally, and physically similar to a normal human but is devoid of conscious EXPERIENCE in the sense of "experience" that requires qualia. Chalmers's Naturalistic Dualism is a version of dualism insofar as it denies that qualia logically supervene on physical processes (*see* SUPERVENIENCE). Chalmers's Naturalistic Dualism is a version of NATURALISM insofar as it posits natural laws that relate qualia to certain physical processes. Further, Chalmers speculates that the physical processes that are important for qualia are physical processes involved in the carrying of INFORMATION. Chalmers ends up embracing a kind of PANPSYCHISM, since information can be found just about anywhere that there are causal interactions. One of the upshots of Chalmers's information-based panpsychism is that it serves as a basis for a defense of the possibility of genuine ARTIFICIAL INTELLIGENCE.

Churchland, Patricia. *Neurophilosophy* **(1986).** This book introduced the term "NEUROPHILOSOPHY" to the world. Churchland is motivated by a version of NATURALISM that emphasizes the continuity of concerns between neuroscience and the philosophy of mind. A large first portion of the book serves as an overview of key findings in neuroscience. The remaining portions of the book defend a philosophy of science that embraces *reductionism* (*see* REDUCTION) and applies it to key controversies concerning the mind. Churchland opposes various strains of mind/brain antireductionism, such as those based on appeals to QUALIA and those based on appeals to MULTIPLE REALIZABILITY. The final portion of the book sketches in broad strokes how key aspects of mental function can be understood from a neurocomputational perspective (*see also* CONNECTIONISM).

Dennett, Daniel. *Consciousness Explained* (1991). Dennett defends a version of FUNCTIONALISM about CONSCIOUSNESS as a means of demonstrating the power of NATURALISM and PHYSICALISM and also as a means of avoiding DUALISM. Dennett views dualism as a position on consciousness that must be avoided at all costs because it is simply a way of avoiding giving any EXPLANATION of consciousness. Dennett argues that one of the main obstacles to overcome in achieving a true explanation of consciousness is the myth of the *Cartesian theater*—a single place in the brain where "it all comes together," where diverse pieces of INFORMATION must appear to be witnessed by the self (*see* SELF, THE). Dennett is skeptical about the Cartesian theater for various reasons. One of which is the illicit appeal to a HOMUNCULUS; another involves countervailing evidence that the information processing that supports consciousness is widely distributed both spatially and temporally in the brain; and yet another reason is Dennett's skepticism about the existence of the self. Dennett holds instead that the self is a kind of fiction, a "center of narrative gravity" that arises in the stories we tell about ourselves—stories with both a nonexistent main character and a nonexistent author. For more on the positive view of consciousness that Dennett articulates in *Consciousness Explained*, see the entry on the MULTIPLE-DRAFTS THEORY OF CONSCIOUSNESS.

Descartes, René. *Meditations on First Philosophy* (1641). Though Descartes is concerned, in this work, with various topics such as the existence of God and our knowledge of the external world, the aspects of central significance to the philosophy of mind are Descartes's treatment of the MIND/BODY PROBLEM and arguments for substance dualism (*see* DUALISM, SUBSTANCE). Building on the certainty about the mind expressed in the COGITO, Descartes argues that he has a clear and distinct conception of himself as a thing that thinks (*see* RES COGITANS), a SUBSTANCE that has the attributes of thinking but none of the attributes of material things. Descartes's denial that the *res cogitans* has any material attributes is based on the SKEPTICAL HYPOTHESIS that a deceitful demon could fool him about the existence of any material objects. If a thinking thing were material, then its existence would lack the certainty previously established in the cogito. Descartes also argues that he has a clear and distinct idea of material substances, RES EXTENSA, as essentially extended and unthinking. Descartes then proceeds to articulate a version of the MODAL ARGUMENT that infers from the CONCEIVABILITY of the distinctness of mind and body to the real

POSSIBILITY of the distinctness of mind and body. One problematic feature of Descartes's line of reasoning is that it depends on the existence of God (a benevolent, nondeceiving creator) as a guarantor of the accuracy of whatever Descartes conceives clearly and distinctly. Without such a guarantee, the objection may be raised that Descartes's clear and distinct *conception* of a distinction is consistent with a lack, in *reality*, of any distinction.

Fodor, Jerry. *The Language of Thought* (1975). This book constitutes a defense of the LANGUAGE OF THOUGHT hypothesis, approaching the topic by showing what the structure of the mind must be if the general gist of the disciplines that make up COGNITIVE SCIENCE—especially *cognitive psychology*—are on the right track in regarding cognition as COMPUTATION. Early in the book, Fodor attacks two kinds of reductionism (*see* REDUCTION). The first attempts to reduce mental states to behavioral dispositions (*see* BEHAVIORISM) and the second attempts to reduce mental states to neurophysiological states (*see* TYPE-IDENTITY THESIS). Among Fodor's attacks on reductionism is an appeal to MULTIPLE REALIZABILITY. Though antireductionist, Fodor's position is still a version of PHYSICALISM, and he affirms a version of the TOKEN-IDENTITY THESIS. These attacks serve to clear room for cognitive psychology to stand as a discipline unto itself. Fodor regards the main entities and processes of cognitive psychology to be PROPOSITIONAL ATTITUDES and the transitions between different propositional attitudes that constitute episodes of INFERENCE. Fodor posits the language of thought to serve as an inner medium for these entities and processes. He thus endorses the existence of a *private language* (*see* PRIVATE-LANGUAGE ARGUMENT). Fodor augments his philosophical arguments for the language of thought with evidence from linguistics and psychology.

Ryle, Gilbert. *The Concept of Mind* (1949). Ryle's book is a sustained attack of the view of the mind as a thing that relates to the body as would a "ghost in the machine," to use the phrase Ryle devised to caricature the central dogma of DESCARTES's substance dualism and similar views (*see* DUALISM, SUBSTANCE). In *The Concept of Mind*, Ryle also defends a view of the mind that many have interpreted as a form of BEHAVIORISM, though such an interpretation is difficult to be sure of (another interpretation is that Ryle holds to a form of FUNCTIONALISM). One relatively well-known strategy of Ryle's is to accuse dualists of committing a kind of mistake that Ryle referred to as a CATEGORY MISTAKE. Another relatively well-known strategy Ryle employed was to accuse his opponents of holding a kind of *intellectualism* that threatened an infinite regress. One way of seeing how the regress was supposed to arise is by supposing that everything that is done intelligently must be accompanied by some episode of thinking. The regress arises because thinking itself is something that can be done either intelligently or unintelligently. But if *everything* that is done intelligently requires the existence of some separate episode of thinking, then insofar as thinking itself is something that is done intelligently, requiring that intelligent behavior be accompanied by one episode of thinking regresses to requiring an infinite number of episodes of thinking. Ryle's recommendation for breaking the regress was to emphasize an analysis of KNOW-HOW that could underwrite the intelligence of intelligent action without itself, the know-how, being some separate intellectual act.

Sellars, Wilfrid. "Empiricism and the Philosophy of Mind" (1956). Originally published as an essay, this best-known work of Sellars's was later released as a stand-alone volume (edited by Richard Rorty and Robert Brandom). Sellars's main focus here is to attack what he called the "MYTH OF THE GIVEN," the empiricist (see EMPIRICISM) doctrine that sensory impressions are nonconceptual yet serve as basic instances of KNOWLEDGE (see SENSATION; NONCONCEPTUAL CONTENT). In addition to attacking the myth of the given, Sellars developed an early version of FUNCTIONALISM that involves applying his brand of SCIENTIFIC REALISM to commonsense psychology (see FOLK PSYCHOLOGY). Sellars develops the view that thoughts (see THOUGHT) and sensory impressions are theoretical posits as opposed to givens. The positing of such entities was not something done in our own lifetime, however, but instead long ago. Sellars illustrates both how such entities may have been posited and how the forms of linguistic practice referring to them may have been passed down to subsequent generations in a way that also accounts for our PRIVILEGED ACCESS to our own mental states. Sellars's key illustrations are given in his discussions of "our Rylean ancestors" (see Gilbert RYLE) and the "myth of Jones" wherein Sellars sketches how a population that understands its members solely in terms of physical and behavioral descriptions can augment its vocabulary to include descriptions of mental states. Such augmentation is done by drawing analogies to certain features of language, especially its semantic and inferential features. Sentences in a language thus serve as a model for mental states such as thoughts. The models for sensory impressions are replicas that resemble that which they are replicas of. In being trained to automatically apply the items of this new vocabulary to their own states, our Rylean ancestors thus come to be able to say that they have various mental states without basing these claims on observations of their own behavior. This automatic application of terms to oneself is the basis, according to Sellars, of a kind of privileged access.

Tye, Michael. *Ten Problems of Consciousness* (1995). Tye defends a version of FIRST-ORDER REPRESENTATIONALISM about phenomenal consciousness (*see* CONSCIOUSNESS, PHENOMENAL)—his PANIC theory of phenomenal character (*see* QUALIA). "PANIC" is an acronym indicating that phenomenal character is one and the same as Poised Abstract Nonconceptual Intentional Content (*see* CONTENT; NONCONCEPTUAL CONTENT; INTENTIONALITY). That is, qualia are one and the same as nonconceptual contents that are abstract, meaning that they concern UNIVERSALS, and poised, meaning that they are available for uptake by systems responsible for BELIEF and DESIRE. Tye develops his case for his PANIC theory by discussing the following ten problems of consciousness. *1. The problem of ownership:* Why do conscious experiences always belong to someone? *2. The problem of perspectival subjectivity:* Why does someone have to have experienced red in order to know WHAT IT IS LIKE to experience red? *3. The problem of mechanism:* How do the objective physical processes in a brain give rise to subjective conscious experiences? *4. The problem of phenomenal causation:* How do the subjective aspects of conscious EXPERIENCE figure into causal explanations? *5. The problem of super blindsight:* What's the difference between a normal subject of phenomenally conscious experiences and a hypothetical subject who forms beliefs without visual qualia about what she looks at? *6. The problem of duplicates:* Could there be a ZOMBIE? *7. The problem of the inverted spectrum:* Could there be an INVERTED SPECTRUM? *8. The problem of transparency:* Why do our conscious experiences exhibit the phenomenon of transparency? (*See* TRANSPARENCY (OF EXPERIENCE)). *9. The problem of felt location and phenomenal vocabulary:* Why would it be incorrect to say of a person with a pain in his/her finger and that finger in his/her mouth that he/she thereby has a pain in his/her mouth? *10. The problem of the alien limb:* How is it that some people can experience their own body parts as no longer belonging to them?

Guide to Further Reading

Introductory overviews of the philosophy of mind

- Churchland, P. M. (1984). *Matter and Consciousness*. Cambridge, MA: MIT Press.
- Rey, G. (1997). *Contemporary Philosophy of Mind: A Contentiously Classical Approach*. Oxford: Blackwell.

Collections of readings in the philosophy of mind

- Rosenthal, D. ed. (1991). *The Nature of Mind*. Oxford: Oxford University Press.
- Lycan, W. and Prinz, J. eds. (2008). *Mind and Cognition: An Anthology, 3rd Edition*. Oxford: Wiley-Blackwell.
- Chalmers, D. ed. (2002). *Philosophy of Mind: Classical and Contemporary Readings*. Oxford: Oxford University Press.

Introductions to consciousness

- Alter, T. A. and Howell, R. (2009). *A Dialogue on Consciousness*. Oxford: Oxford University Press.
- Seager, W. (1999). *Theories of Consciousness: An Introduction and Assessment*. New York: Routledge.

Introductions to intentionality and mental representation

- Cummins, R. (1989). *Meaning and Mental Representation*. Cambridge, MA: MIT Press.
- Clapin, H. ed. (2002). *Philosophy of Mental Representation*. Oxford: Oxford University Press.

Introductions to cognitive science and its philosophical foundations

- Clark, A. (2001). *Mindware: An Introduction to the Philosophy of Cognitive Science*. Oxford: Oxford University Press.
- Kolak, D., Hirstein, W., Mandik, P., and Waskan, J. (2006). *Cognitive Science: An Introduction to Mind and Brain*. New York: Routledge.

Index

Numbers in bold indicate location of definition of term or biography of person.